Reading Comprehension Test Taking Skills Grade 2

Best Value Books™

by
Patricia Pedigo
and
Dr. Roger DeSanti

Copyright © 1998, Carson-Dellosa Publishing Company, Inc., Greensboro, North Carolina 27425, publishers of the "Stick Out Your Neck" series. All rights reserved. The purchase of this material entitles the buyer to reproduce worksheets and activities for classroom use only—not for commercial resale. Reproduction of these materials for an entire school or district is prohibited. No part of this book may be reproduced (except as noted above), stored in a retrieval system, or transmitted in any form or by any means (mechanically, electronically, recording, etc.) without the prior written consent of Carson-Dellosa Publishing Co., Inc.

ISBN 0-88724-475-0

Table of Contents

Word Skills
Reading Words
Test 1 1
Test 2 2
Test 3 3
Test 4 4
Test 5 5
Test 6 6
Test 7 7
Test 8 8
Test 9 9
Test 10 10
Test 11 11
Test 12 12
Test 13 13

Word Study Skills
Test 1 14
Test 2 15
Test 3 16
Test 4 17
Test 5 18
Test 6 19
Test 7 20
Test 8 21
Test 9 22

Spelling
Test 1 23
Test 2 24
Test 3 25
Test 4 26
Test 5 27
Test 6 28
Test 7 29
Test 8 30
Test 9 31

Synonyms
Test 1 32
Test 2 33
Test 3 34
Test 4 35
Test 5 36
Test 6 37

Synonyms (continued)
Test 7 38
Test 8 39
Test 9 40

Antonyms
Test 1 41
Test 2 42
Test 3 43
Test 4 44
Test 5 45
Test 6 46
Test 7 47
Test 8 48
Test 9 49

Vocabulary
Test 1 50
Test 2 51
Test 3 52
Test 4 53
Test 5 54
Test 6 55
Test 7 56
Test 8 57
Test 9 58
Test 10 59
Test 11 60
Test 12 61
Test 13 62

Comprehension
Reading Sentences
Tent, Skiing 63
Kangaroo, Bird 64
Octopus, Frog 65
Apple, Test 66
Giraffe, Skates 67
Parrot, Owl 68
Castle, Zebra 69
Town, Painting 70
Music, Rainbow 71
Bees, Raccoon 72
Rabbit, Circus 73
Thanksgiving, Ball 74
Stars, House 75

Narrative Passages
Eating Cookies,
    Best Friend 76
Fall Leaves, Bike Riding . .77
Go Slow, New Baby 78
Treehouse,
    Dancing Lessons 79
Puppies,
    Crossing the Street 80
Pizza Day, Being Small . .81
Collecting Rocks,
    The Pond 82
Magic Trick, Store Visit . . .83
New Girl at School,
    Growing Seeds 84
Shine My Shoes,
    Getting Wet 85
A Bad Day, Ted the Taxi . .86

Expository Passages
Community, Police 87
Firefighters, Doctors 88
Dentists, Farmers 89
Storekeepers, Neighbors .90
Restaurant, School 91
Library, Hospital 92
Body, Heart 93
Lungs, Stomach 94
Brain, Parts of the Body . .95
Health, Exercise 96
Germs, Clothes 97
Teeth, Medicine 98

Letters
Peg, Lyle 99
Mr. White, Aunt Alice . . .100
Bob, Mr. Broom 101
Mom, Phil 102
Susan, Grandma 103
Elmer, Julie 104

About the book

This book is just one in our Best Value™ series of reproducible, skill-oriented activity books. Standardized tests have become a typical means of student achievement evaluation. Many students may not perform as well as they might on these tests simply due to a lack of practice in test taking and/or a lack of understanding of the task presented. This book is designed to provide practice activities for appropriate application of reading comprehension and test taking strategies.

The passages presented in this book cover a variety of word skills and real reading situations including narrative, expository, directions, and letters. The passage questions are presented in a typical standardized testing format that targets specific levels of comprehension (literal, inferential, applied, and prediction or judgmental). Each level of comprehension calls for different strategies that are discussed in detail on the pages titled "Levels of Comprehension." It is the authors' contention that children should be made aware of these levels of comprehension and the associated strategies for each. Providing the children with these comprehension tools gives them an organized approach to answering questions about any given passage.

Also included in this book is a list of Test Taking Tips for students, found on page vi. This list includes many strategies that may be helpful in a variety of test taking situations (true and false, multiple choice, and matching).

About the authors

Patricia Pedigo has many years of teaching experience in urban, rural, public, and private settings. She has taught all elementary and middle school grade levels and has been a reading specialist. While teaching at the University of New Orleans, Patricia professed her belief in finding creative ways to teach through practical applications. She has created many materials that incorporate a reading approach integrating content areas and language development. She holds an M.Ed. in Reading Education.

Dr. Roger DeSanti has been an educator since the mid 1970's. His teaching experiences have spanned a wide range of grade and ability levels from deaf nursery through university graduate school. As a professor, he has authored numerous articles and books, achievement tests, and instructional materials.

Levels of Comprehension

There are many levels at which we may comprehend text, ranging from very simple to deeply complex. There are several different models of comprehension that demonstrate these levels in a detailed manner. However, we found that a simple version of these models is most effective with children. Below is a short passage followed by a discussion of four levels of comprehension, example questions, and strategies to employ when answering the questions.

> **Ben sat on the front steps. His chin was cupped in his hand and tears were trickling down his cheeks. On the step beside Ben lay a leash with the name "Rags" embossed on the leather. Ben had looked everywhere he could think, but it was no use.**

Literal

Literal comprehension is an understanding of what has been clearly stated in the passage. Questions that require literal comprehension will ask for information that has been given. For example:

1. What is the name of the boy in this story? (Ben)
2. Where is Ben sitting? (on the front steps)
3. What is on the step next to Ben? (a leash)

The best strategy for answering literal comprehension questions is simply to look back at the text and find the answer.

Inferential

Inferential comprehension is the ability to understand the implied message of the text. Questions that require inferential comprehension will ask for information that is suggested but never directly stated in the text. For example:

1. How is Ben feeling? (sad)

To answer an inferential comprehension question the reader needs to find clues that imply the meaning. For the example question, it is necessary to look at the stated information that gives a hint as to how Ben may be feeling. The example states that Ben's "chin was cupped in his hand," a behavior that usually accompanies boredom or sadness. The second clue given is that "tears were trickling down his cheeks." These two pieces of information imply that Ben is sad.

Levels of Comprehension

> Ben sat on the front steps. His chin was cupped in his hand and tears were trickling down his cheeks. On the step beside Ben lay a leash with the name "Rags" embossed on the leather. Ben had looked everywhere he could think, but it was no use.

Applied

Applied comprehension requires that the reader use the stated and implied information and apply it to what he/she already knows about such situations. This level of comprehension takes the reader beyond the text and into his/her own knowledge base. For example:

1. Who is Rags? (a dog, cat, or other pet)
2. Why do you think Ben is sad? (He cannot find Rags.)

To answer an applied comprehension question the reader must extract the stated and implied information, compare and contrast it to his/her general knowledge, and arrive at a logical conclusion. To answer question number one, it is necessary to understand that: the name "Rags" is embossed on the leash (stated information); Ben cares about Rags (implied information); and that leashes are used for walking pets (general knowledge). To answer question number two, it is necessary to understand that: Ben had been looking for something (stated information); he could not find what he was looking for (implied information); Rags is probably what is missing (implied); and lost pets often make children sad (general knowledge).

Judgmental

Judgmental comprehension is the level at which the reader can process the information to arrive at an opinion or prediction that can be justified or supported with facts. For example:

1. What else might Ben do to find Rags?

To answer a judgmental comprehension question the reader must form an opinion or prediction that is logical to the story. There may be many acceptable answers, but they must be supported by the facts from the story and/or real life situations. For example, a child may answer, "I would put up posters of Rags with my phone number. That is what my friend did when she lost her dog. Ben wants to find Rags and the neighbors might be able to help."

Test Taking Tips

True and False
- Read the question carefully. If any part is false, mark the answer false.
- Look for key words like the words listed below. Think about what the words mean.

    always   only   never   all
    usually   every   frequently   often

Multiple Choice
- Read the question carefully. See if you know the answer <u>before</u> you look at the choices.
- Read <u>all</u> the choices, even if the first choice seems right.
- If you don't know which answer is correct, cross out the answers you know are <u>wrong</u>. Then, pick from the choices that are left.
- Always put down an answer. If you leave it blank, you know it is wrong. A guess might be right!

Matching
- Match the answers you know first.
- When you've made a match, cross out the number so you know it has been used.
- If you aren't sure, guess!

Ready-To-Use Ideas and Activities

The activities in this book will help children master the basic skills necessary to become competent test takers. Remember, as you read through the activities listed below, and as you go through this book, that all children learn at their own rate. Although repetition is important, it is critical that we never lose sight of the fact that it is equally important to build children's self-esteem and self-confidence if we want them to become successful learners.

Practice Test Taking
Reproduce the pages in this book to administer as a test to the students. Answers should be marked by completely darkening the "bubble" next to the selected choice. Practice tests may be administered in various ways: You may wish to select one practice sheet from each skill and give each student a "packet" similar to the standardized testing procedure. When the students are familiar with the practice test format, give them a practice timed test as most standardized tests are timed. It is suggested that three to five minutes be given for each page and that no test packet should exceed twenty minutes. You may also use the book as practice to reinforce particular skills.

Flash Cards
The back of this book has removable flash cards that will be great for use in basic skill and enrichment activities. Pull the flash cards out and cut them apart. If you have access to a paper cutter, use it to cut the flash cards apart. The following is just one of the ways you may want to use these flash cards.

Reproduce the bingo sheet on the next page in this book, making enough copies to have one for each student. Hand them out to the students. Take the flash cards and write the words on the chalk board. Have the students choose 24 of the words and write them in any order on the empty spaces of their bingo cards, writing only one word in each space. When all students have finished their cards, take the flash cards and make them into a deck. Call out the words one at a time. Any student who has a word that is called out should make an "X" through the word to cross it out. The first student who crosses out five words in a row (horizontally, vertically, or diagonally) wins the game. To extend the game, continue playing until a student crosses out all the words on his bingo sheet.

Name _____   Skill: Reading Words—Test 2

DIRECTIONS:
Look at each picture. Then, mark the word that best describes the picture on each line below it.

1. park   present   press
   ○   ○   ○
2. bone   bow   back
   ○   ○   ○
3. ribbon robin   ran
   ○   ○   ○

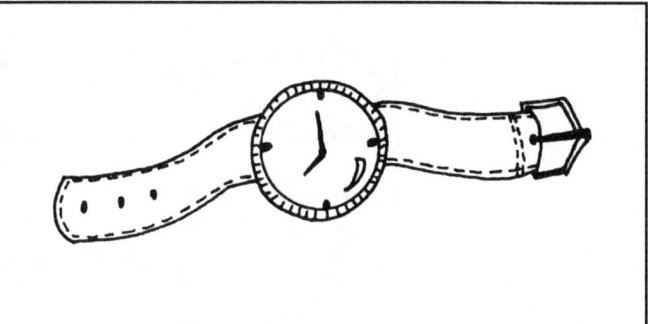

7. watch   witch   with
   ○   ○   ○
8. had   happy   hands
   ○   ○   ○
9. Tim   tore   time
   ○   ○   ○

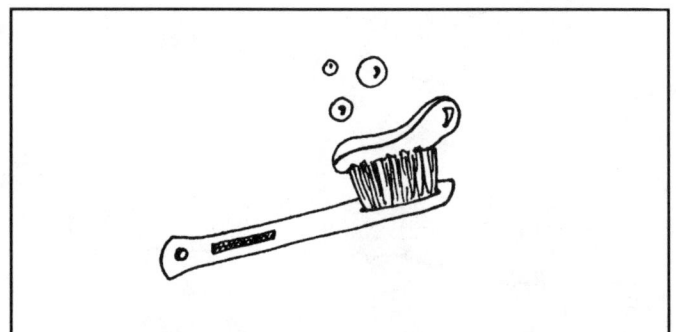

4. brush   bush   brave
   ○   ○   ○
5. pan   past   paste
   ○   ○   ○
6. teeth   told   tack
   ○   ○   ○

10. trick   truck   tractor
    ○   ○   ○
11. frame   farmer   fall
    ○   ○   ○
12. tires   trim   tells
    ○   ○   ○

Name _____

Skill: Reading Words—Test 3

DIRECTIONS:
Look at each picture. Then, mark the word that best describes the picture on each line below it.

1. glad   globe   gone
   ○   ○   ○
2. world   worm   wall
   ○   ○   ○
3. Earth   Mars   sun
   ○   ○   ○

7. boat   airplane   arm
   ○   ○   ○
8. clip   could   clouds
   ○   ○   ○
9. sack   skip   sky
   ○   ○   ○

4. scarf   scare   sold
   ○   ○   ○
5. cold   cost   class
   ○   ○   ○
6. mittens   mind   kittens
   ○   ○   ○

10. pal   puppy   pony
    ○   ○   ○
11. bare   bone   blow
    ○   ○   ○
12. wag   wig   win
    ○   ○   ○

© Carson-Dellosa CD-3734

Name _____   Skill: Reading Words—Test 4

DIRECTIONS:
Look at each picture. Then, mark the word that best describes the picture on each line below it.

1. drag   deer   dinosaur   7. rink   rang   ring
   ○   ○   ○   ○   ○   ○
2. taste   tail   trail   8. stone   stamp   slap
   ○   ○   ○   ○   ○   ○
3. huge   hug   hop   9. city   round   come
   ○   ○   ○   ○   ○   ○

 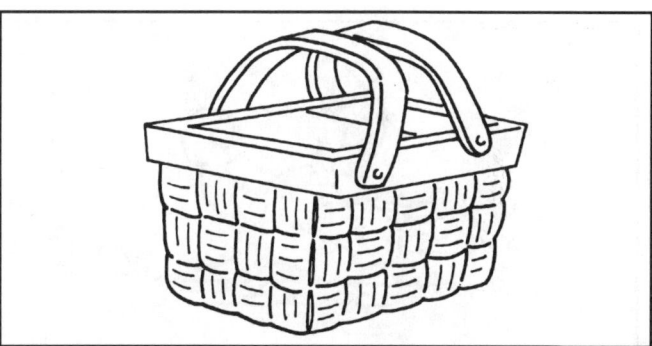

4. from   frog   fold   10. basket base   blade
   ○   ○   ○   ○   ○   ○
5. pole   poor   pond   11. part   picnic pick
   ○   ○   ○   ○   ○   ○
6. flew   flower feel   12. lamp   land   lunch
   ○   ○   ○   ○   ○   ○

© Carson-Dellosa CD-3734

Name _____

Skill: Reading Words—Test 5

DIRECTIONS:
Look at each picture. Then, mark the word that best describes the picture on each line below it.

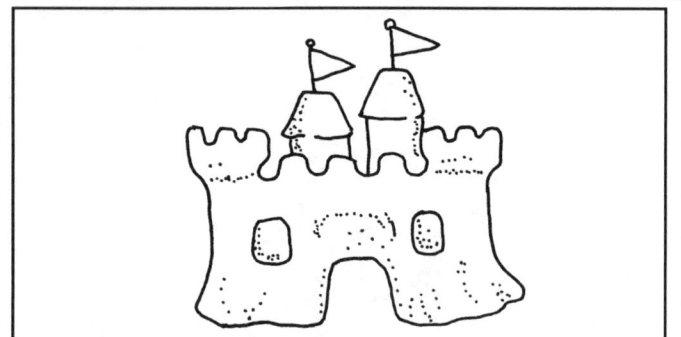

1. castle   cast   cake
   ○   ○   ○
2. flew   flow   flag
   ○   ○   ○
3. sit   stone sand
   ○   ○   ○

7. crow   cow   call
   ○   ○   ○
8. spots   stops   spark
   ○   ○   ○
9. hold   horns   hall
   ○   ○   ○

4. candy   crab   cream
   ○   ○   ○
5. cape   claw   clue
   ○   ○   ○
6. swim   swing   sip
   ○   ○   ○

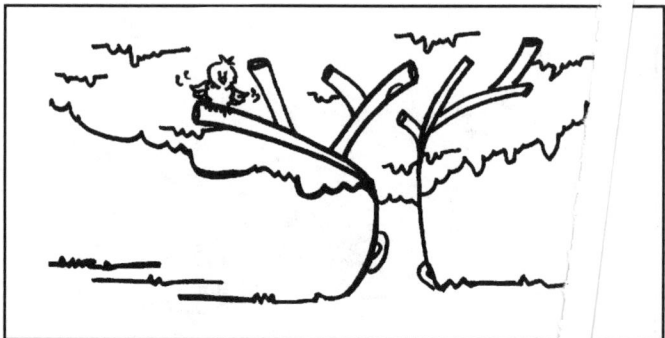

10. try   trim   tree
    ○   ○   ○
11. broke   branch bank
    ○   ○   ○
12. leaves lift   nd
    ○   ○   ○

© Carson-Dellosa CD-3734

Name _____

Skill: Reading Words—Test 6

DIRECTIONS:
Look at each picture. Then, mark the word that best describes the picture on each line below it.

1. elephant egg end
   ○　　　　○　　○
2. trick tank trunk
   ○　　　○　　○
3. spin splash slap
   ○　　　○　　　○

7. July January June
   ○　　　○　　　○
8. month moth mother
   ○　　　○　　　○
9. dent date damp
   ○　　　○　　　○

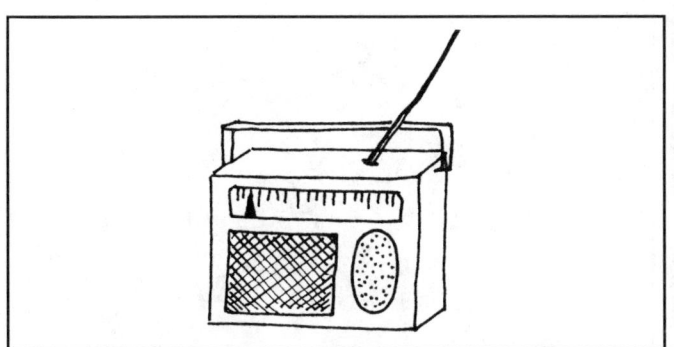

4. radio road ramp
   ○　　　○　　○
5. mouth music maps
   ○　　　○　　○
6. plan past play
   ○　　　○　　○

10. bench branch beach
    ○　　　○　　　○
11. under uncle umbrella
    ○　　　○　　　○
12. warm well wing
    ○　　　○　　○

© Carson-Dellosa CD-3734

Name _____

Skill: Reading Words—Test 7

DIRECTIONS:
Look at each picture. Then, mark the word that best describes the picture on each line below it.

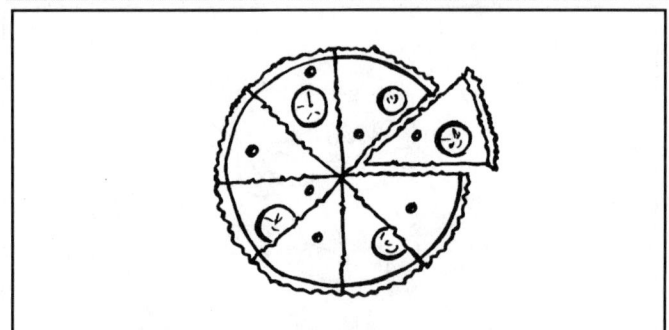

1. pillow   pretty   pizza
   ○   ○   ○

2. safe   slip   slice
   ○   ○   ○

3. rope   robe   round
   ○   ○   ○

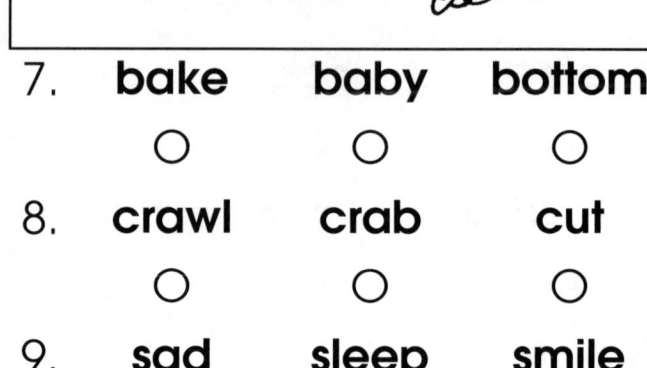

7. bake   baby   bottom
   ○   ○   ○

8. crawl   crab   cut
   ○   ○   ○

9. sad   sleep   smile
   ○   ○   ○

4. shell   swim   swing
   ○   ○   ○

5. empty   else   eight
   ○   ○   ○

6. three   four   five
   ○   ○   ○

10. pick   picture pants
    ○   ○   ○

11. cap   cup   cape
    ○   ○   ○

12. bend   bag   boy
    ○   ○   ○

© Carson-Dellosa CD-3734

Name _____

Skill: Reading Words—Test 8

DIRECTIONS:
Look at each picture. Then, mark the word that best describes the picture on each line below it.

1. hoop   hold   house
   ○   ○   ○
2. rope   roof   root
   ○   ○   ○
3. smoke smile smell
   ○   ○   ○

7. crown crow   cart
   ○   ○   ○
8. pond   point paint
   ○   ○   ○
9. quite squirrel queen
   ○   ○   ○

4. almost any   apple
   ○   ○   ○
5. fruit   friend file
   ○   ○   ○
6. leaf   left   laugh
   ○   ○   ○

10. sail   snail snap
    ○   ○   ○
11. shell shall sell
    ○   ○   ○
12. slow   slid   slept
    ○   ○   ○

Name _____   Skill: Reading Words—Test 9

DIRECTIONS:
Look at each picture. Then, mark the word that best describes the picture on each line below it.

1. worm   warm   wand
   ○   ○   ○
2. grew   gas   grass
   ○   ○   ○
3. crawl   claw   clap
   ○   ○   ○

7. start   store   still
   ○   ○   ○
8. fruit   feet   fort
   ○   ○   ○
9. sing   sign   sand
   ○   ○   ○

4. rake   rabbit reach
   ○   ○   ○
5. fold   furry   find
   ○   ○   ○
6. can   cart   carrot
   ○   ○   ○

10. chip   children chicken
    ○   ○   ○
11. fence family foot
    ○   ○   ○
12. will   wand   wing
    ○   ○   ○

© Carson-Dellosa CD-3734

Name _____   Skill: Reading Words—Test 10

DIRECTIONS:
Look at each picture. Then, mark the word that best describes the picture on each line below it.

1. school   scare   should
   ○   ○   ○
2. gift   grill   girl
   ○   ○   ○
3. circle   chew   child
   ○   ○   ○

7. lead   late   ladder
   ○   ○   ○
8. stops   shall   steps
   ○   ○   ○
9. high   hang   held
   ○   ○   ○

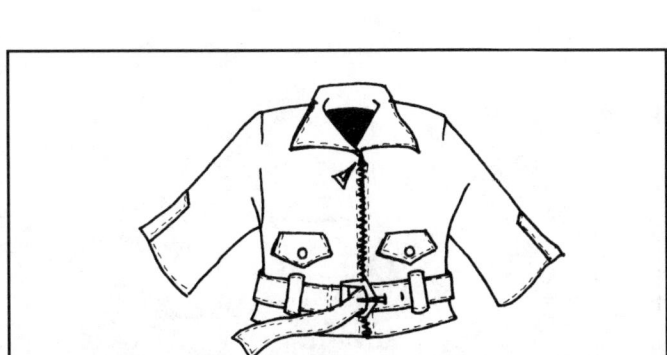

4. jacks   jacket   jet
   ○   ○   ○
5. belt   bold   band
   ○   ○   ○
6. pack   pond   pocket
   ○   ○   ○

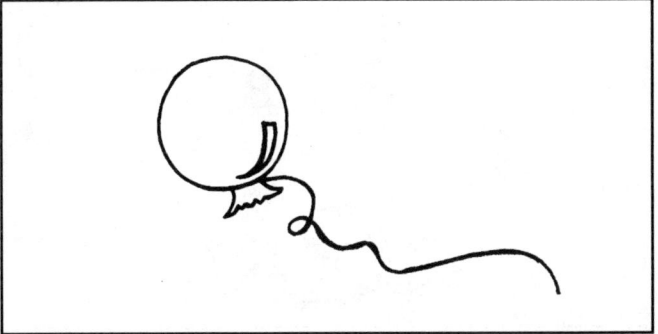

10. balloon   barn   bend
    ○   ○   ○
11. sting   string   stripe
    ○   ○   ○
12. roller   rooster round
    ○   ○   ○

© Carson-Dellosa CD-3734

Name _____   Skill: Reading Words—Test 11

DIRECTIONS:
Look at each picture. Then, mark the word that best describes the picture on each line below it.

1. cone   camp   camel
   ○   ○   ○

7. egg   each   enter
   ○   ○   ○

2. hand   hum   humps
   ○   ○   ○

8. blew   bread   broken
   ○   ○   ○

3. wing   walk   wake
   ○   ○   ○

9. share   shall   shell
   ○   ○   ○

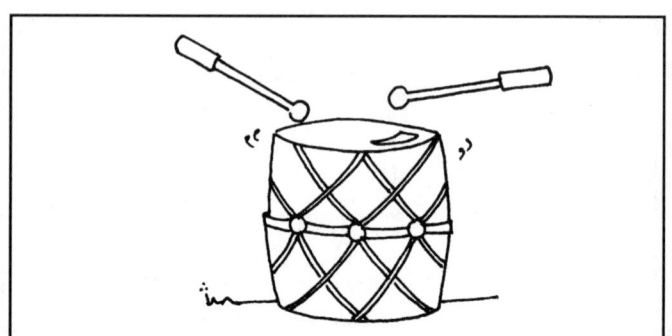

4. drum   drag   dug
   ○   ○   ○

10. butterfly butter   band
    ○   ○   ○

5. bull   bank   bang
   ○   ○   ○

11. flour   flower   floor
    ○   ○   ○

6. loud   cloud   lake
   ○   ○   ○

12. spell   spring   spin
    ○   ○   ○

© Carson-Dellosa CD-3734

Name _____   Skill: Reading Words—Test 12

DIRECTIONS:
Look at each picture. Then, mark the word that best describes the picture on each line below it.

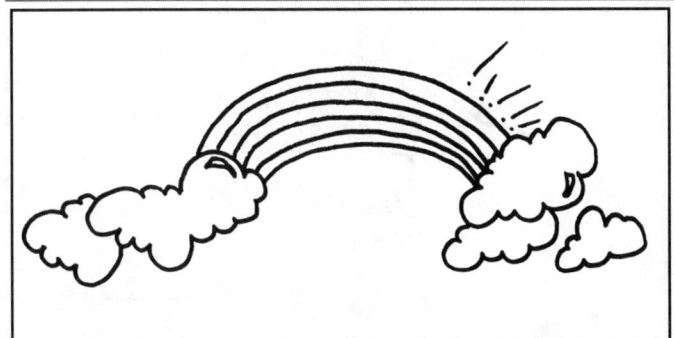

1. ramp   rainbow   rate
   ○   ○   ○
2. colors   coat   care
   ○   ○   ○
3. clamp   clouds   could
   ○   ○   ○

7. test   tell   tent
   ○   ○   ○
8. cream   camp   cast
   ○   ○   ○
9. yard   year   yell
   ○   ○   ○

4. both   boy   bare
   ○   ○   ○
5. sing   sand   sun
   ○   ○   ○
6. almost add   alone
   ○   ○   ○

10. pool   pile   pond
    ○   ○   ○
11. float flap   fire
    ○   ○   ○
12. state space   splash
    ○   ○   ○

© Carson-Dellosa CD-3734

Name _____

Skill: Reading Words—Test 13

DIRECTIONS:
Look at each picture. Then, mark the word that best describes the picture on each line below it.

1. dollar   donkey   duck
   ○   ○   ○
2. felt   feathers family
   ○   ○   ○
3. swim   sunny   super
   ○   ○   ○

7. lean   lend   lamp
   ○   ○   ○
8. flew   flap   fall
   ○   ○   ○
9. crash   crayon   candle
   ○   ○   ○

4. gate   grape   giant
   ○   ○   ○
5. hard   huge   hung
   ○   ○   ○
6. grab   gotten   girl
   ○   ○   ○

10. owl   own   open
    ○   ○   ○
11. week   wing   wire
    ○   ○   ○
12. bird   building bump
    ○   ○   ○

© Carson-Dellosa CD-3734

Name _____   Skill: Word Study—Test 3

DIRECTIONS:
One or more letters are underlined in each of the words below. Read each word, then mark the space under the answer choice that has the same sound as the underlined letter or letters.

1. ba<u>nk</u>			8. <u>a</u>rm		
both ○	pink ○	been ○	chain ○	farmer ○	clam ○

2. co<u>st</u>			9. <u>fr</u>ee		
stair ○	cats ○	count ○	tree ○	form ○	frame ○

3. dra<u>g</u>on			10. p<u>a</u>ste		
get ○	giant ○	drum ○	past ○	star ○	mate ○

4. <u>on</u>ce			11. m<u>oo</u>		
tone ○	won ○	no ○	you ○	mouth ○	put ○

5. ba<u>nd</u>			12. enou<u>gh</u>		
lend ○	bent ○	slap ○	give ○	fall ○	goat ○

6. be<u>y</u>ond			13. ran<u>ch</u>		
yellow ○	win ○	jog ○	ramp ○	chip ○	clip ○

7. bree<u>z</u>e			14. dogh<u>ou</u>se		
extra ○	smile ○	easy ○	hose ○	mouth ○	poor ○

© Carson-Dellosa CD-3734

Name _____   Skill: Word Study—Test 4

DIRECTIONS:
One or more letters are underlined in each of the words below. Read each word, then mark the space under the answer choice that has the same sound as the underlined letter or letters.

1. clo<u>th</u>			8. <u>e</u>mpty		
close ○	math ○	string ○	they ○	send ○	them ○

2. ch<u>ir</u>p			9. c<u>o</u>rn		
big ○	bird ○	chip ○	morning ○	hour ○	rub ○

3. ca<u>g</u>e			10. blo<u>ck</u>		
catch ○	orange ○	get ○	climb ○	catch ○	cricket ○

4. <u>k</u>nee			11. ma<u>r</u>k		
cow ○	kite ○	can ○	pick ○	part ○	pork ○

5. pro<u>bl</u>em			12. <u>qu</u>ack		
blend ○	ball ○	bold ○	crack ○	squirrel ○	hunt ○

6. dr<u>u</u>m			13. <u>p</u>lain		
burn ○	umbrella ○	drag ○	play ○	rain ○	pal ○

7. <u>p</u>ress			14. a<u>s</u>leep		
grass ○	part ○	prune ○	slip ○	silk ○	also ○

© Carson-Dellosa CD-3734

Name _____   Skill: Word Study—Test 5

DIRECTIONS:
One or more letters are underlined in each of the words below. Read each word, then mark the space under the answer choice that has the same sound as the underlined letter or letters.

1. again<u>st</u>
   - slap ○
   - ago ○
   - past ○

2. c<u>an</u>dle
   - cane ○
   - lamp ○
   - pan ○

3. pr<u>ou</u>d
   - pond ○
   - pool ○
   - loud ○

4. bo<u>ss</u>
   - grass ○
   - boat ○
   - stamp ○

5. mi<u>lk</u>
   - silk ○
   - pure ○
   - take ○

6. bod<u>y</u>
   - meet ○
   - play ○
   - try ○

7. colle<u>ct</u>
   - fact ○
   - fake ○
   - rock ○

8. de<u>sk</u>
   - skate ○
   - sake ○
   - shape ○

9. ch<u>in</u>
   - chip ○
   - moon ○
   - hit ○

10. ba<u>sk</u>et
    - shake ○
    - scare ○
    - test ○

11. ke<u>pt</u>
    - kit ○
    - pat ○
    - slept ○

12. p<u>ay</u>
    - pad ○
    - part ○
    - made ○

13. art<u>ist</u>
    - slap ○
    - stop ○
    - sand ○

14. <u>th</u>in
    - both ○
    - tin ○
    - hit ○

Name _____   Skill: Word Study—Test 6

DIRECTIONS:
One or more letters are underlined in each of the words below. Read each word, then mark the space under the answer choice that has the same sound as the underlined letter or letters.

1. sw_a_m			8. bl_ew_		
win ○	sweet ○	whisper ○	we ○	blow ○	you ○

2. bri_ng_			9. c_a_se		
tang ○	rang ○	string ○	gain ○	pat ○	kite ○

3. brok_en_			10. _fl_ap		
new ○	enter ○	neck ○	fall ○	half ○	flower ○

4. b_u_g			11. b_or_n		
juice ○	jump ○	bloom ○	hour ○	stomp ○	storm ○

5. j_o_ke			12. d_one_		
hole ○	hop ○	today ○	stone ○	bone ○	under ○

6. sh_y_			13. _b_et		
toy ○	pony ○	cry ○	tab ○	pet ○	top ○

7. b_ea_ch			14. earl_y_		
ten ○	eat ○	bat ○	year ○	eat ○	badly ○

Name _____   Skill: Word Study—Test 7

DIRECTIONS:
One or more letters are underlined in each of the words below. Read each word, then mark the space under the answer choice that has the same sound as the underlined letter or letters.

1. clap

   cap   tap   climb
   ○   ○   ○

2. toe

   not   no   ton
   ○   ○   ○

3. smart

   mist   maps   small
   ○   ○   ○

4. trail

   pail   free   tree
   ○   ○   ○

5. circus

   same   cute   cake
   ○   ○   ○

6. gate

   tale   hang   hat
   ○   ○   ○

7. broke

   top   cold   bottom
   ○   ○   ○

8. dirt

   bird   dark   damp
   ○   ○   ○

9. bang

   bank   ring   grand
   ○   ○   ○

10. purple

    nurse pink   pump
    ○   ○   ○

11. brace

    brand about barn
    ○   ○   ○

12. chicken

    chap   shall socks
    ○   ○   ○

13. tuna

    under put   fruit
    ○   ○   ○

14. cap

    kit   can   pace
    ○   ○   ○

Name _____   Skill: Word Study—Test 8

DIRECTIONS:
One or more letters are underlined in each of the words below. Read each word, then mark the space under the answer choice that has the same sound as the underlined letter or letters.

1. da<u>sh</u>

  shop ○   dip ○   both ○

2. <u>f</u>arm

  phone ○   harm ○   pull ○

3. m<u>ea</u>t

  mat ○   bet ○   beet ○

4. cl<u>ue</u>

  purple ○   pump ○   rule ○

5. bl<u>ow</u>

  top ○   more ○   poke ○

6. le<u>ft</u>

  feel ○   felt ○   lift ○

7. p<u>oi</u>nt

  pool ○   toy ○   spoon ○

8. ca<u>mp</u>

  pan ○   limp ○   came ○

9. <u>sl</u>ide

  asleep ○   sheep ○   lid ○

10. be<u>nd</u>

  bent ○   from ○   friend ○

11. <u>c</u>url

  turkey ○   cramp ○   glad ○

12. bu<u>sh</u>

  fist ○   shut ○   snip ○

13. <u>s</u>pace

  skip ○   wasp ○   sap ○

14. an<u>y</u>

  cry ○   teeth ○   yellow ○

© Carson-Dellosa CD-3734

Name _____   Skill: Spelling—Test 2

DIRECTIONS:
Read each group of words. Mark the one that is **not** spelled correctly.

1. ○ road
   ○ very
   ○ being
   ○ evryone

2. ○ part
   ○ star
   ○ winde
   ○ arrow

3. ○ bike
   ○ eye
   ○ keep
   ○ pickture

4. ○ plan
   ○ stepe
   ○ without
   ○ asleep

5. ○ pot
   ○ stone
   ○ wurd
   ○ awake

6. ○ insied
   ○ pan
   ○ stand
   ○ white

7. ○ sad
   ○ walk
   ○ better
   ○ partey

8. ○ stay
   ○ wish
   ○ artest
   ○ sat

9. ○ bit
   ○ family
   ○ king
   ○ pleese

10. ○ seede
    ○ went
    ○ black
    ○ faster

11. ○ rok
    ○ wait
    ○ best
    ○ isn't

12. ○ start
    ○ wintter
    ○ same
    ○ was

13. ○ water
    ○ brithday
    ○ face
    ○ kind

14. ○ stick
    ○ wood
    ○ aunt
    ○ skool

15. ○ kitten
    ○ pound
    ○ stoore
    ○ worker

Name _____   Skill: Spelling—Test 3

DIRECTIONS:
Read each group of words. Mark the one that is **not** spelled correctly.

1. ○ babby
   ○ show
   ○ were
   ○ boat

2. ○ bone
   ○ felle
   ○ leg
   ○ push

3. ○ reddy
   ○ table
   ○ zoo
   ○ bang

4. ○ small
   ○ won't
   ○ bus
   ○ flor

5. ○ long
   ○ roum
   ○ teacher
   ○ bare

6. ○ feed
   ○ leave
   ○ prety
   ○ story

7. ○ stuk
   ○ yellow
   ○ balloon
   ○ sleep

8. ○ slow
   ○ woman
   ○ brown
   ○ furst

9. ○ line
   ○ right
   ○ talle
   ○ bar

10. ○ wud
    ○ care
    ○ food
    ○ love

11. ○ yel
    ○ backyard
    ○ sing
    ○ when

12. ○ window
    ○ brother
    ○ fine
    ○ ledder

13. ○ ligth
    ○ real
    ○ tail
    ○ bank

14. ○ sume
    ○ work
    ○ cake
    ○ flower

15. ○ rope
    ○ than
    ○ barn
    ○ your'e

Name _____   Skill: Spelling—Test 4

DIRECTIONS:
Read each group of words. Mark the one that is **not** spelled correctly.

1. ○ cave
   ○ gave
   ○ lunnch
   ○ sandy

2. ○ sang
   ○ abouve
   ○ baseball
   ○ street

3. ○ thos
   ○ act
   ○ basket
   ○ need

4. ○ swim
   ○ clos
   ○ gone
   ○ might

5. ○ mixt
   ○ shoe
   ○ told
   ○ against

6. ○ thier
   ○ able
   ○ base
   ○ still

7. ○ children
   ○ glad
   ○ these
   ○ ackross

8. ○ suprise
   ○ gold
   ○ clean
   ○ men

9. ○ seen
   ○ tire
   ○ afrade
   ○ beach

10. ○ talk
    ○ again
    ○ clouwn
    ○ grass

11. ○ youth
    ○ chair
    ○ give
    ○ makeing

12. ○ namme
    ○ class
    ○ mean
    ○ seat

13. ○ sekret
    ○ tiger
    ○ add
    ○ bath

14. ○ next
    ○ take
    ○ cloud
    ○ gramda

15. ○ mom
    ○ shop
    ○ tonite
    ○ age

Name _____   Skill: Spelling—Test 5

DIRECTIONS:
Read each group of words. Mark the one that is **not** spelled correctly.

1. ○ tell
   ○ ago
   ○ great
   ○ monney

2. ○ morning
   ○ shout
   ○ toy
   ○ ahede

3. ○ air
   ○ bedrume
   ○ them
   ○ always

4. ○ another
   ○ cook
   ○ hand
   ○ mouve

5. ○ think
   ○ any
   ○ countree
   ○ head

6. ○ shuld
   ○ town
   ○ agree
   ○ became

7. ○ becum
   ○ that's
   ○ along
   ○ color

8. ○ comming
   ○ guess
   ○ move
   ○ sign

9. ○ sister
   ○ tried
   ○ alike
   ○ befor

10. ○ miself
    ○ six
    ○ alley
    ○ behind

11. ○ thank
    ○ alone
    ○ cold
    ○ greew

12. ○ ground
    ○ moste
    ○ side
    ○ track

13. ○ train
    ○ airplan
    ○ bedtime
    ○ then

14. ○ could'nt
    ○ he's
    ○ six
    ○ trip

15. ○ thought
    ○ cry
    ○ hear
    ○ nammed

Name _____   Skill: Spelling—Test 6

DIRECTIONS:
Read each group of words. Mark the one that is <u>not</u> spelled correctly.

1. ○ smell
   ○ try
   ○ allmost
   ○ believe

2. ○ bell
   ○ tooday
   ○ aren't
   ○ dark

3. ○ nice
   ○ snow
   ○ use
   ○ anser

4. ○ bench
   ○ pick
   ○ tree
   ○ bakke

5. ○ plase
   ○ trick
   ○ bark
   ○ done

6. ○ three
   ○ applle
   ○ dance
   ○ heard

7. ○ helper
   ○ never
   ○ aslo
   ○ belong

8. ○ top
   ○ ate
   ○ doktor
   ○ noise

9. ○ doe'snt
   ○ hold
   ○ hole
   ○ note

10. ○ elefant
    ○ flash
    ○ gotten
    ○ hunt

11. ○ neer
    ○ smile
    ○ turn
    ○ already

12. ○ took
    ○ arund
    ○ dinner
    ○ herself

13. ○ nose
    ○ someday
    ○ was'nt
    ○ anybody

14. ○ somone
    ○ watch
    ○ anymore
    ○ bend

15. ○ leaff
    ○ meat
    ○ beyond
    ○ clear

Name _____   Skill: Spelling—Test 7

DIRECTIONS:
Read each group of words. Mark the one that is **not** spelled correctly.

1. ○ deskt
   ○ flat
   ○ grab
   ○ lean

2. ○ buterfly
   ○ die
   ○ flip
   ○ click

3. ○ ice
   ○ lether
   ○ blew
   ○ buy

4. ○ blok
   ○ cage
   ○ cloth
   ○ dine

5. ○ durt
   ○ enter
   ○ fold
   ○ grown

6. ○ butter
   ○ clever
   ○ else
   ○ fleew

7. ○ grandfather
   ○ learn
   ○ blankat
   ○ button

8. ○ clock
   ○ dig
   ○ enemy
   ○ flud

9. ○ enuff
   ○ flour
   ○ growl
   ○ important

10. ○ indeed
    ○ lemon
    ○ midle
    ○ blow

11. ○ graid
    ○ hurry
    ○ leap
    ○ melt

12. ○ clim
    ○ empty
    ○ different
    ○ float

13. ○ gray
    ○ idea
    ○ ledd
    ○ met

14. ○ left
    ○ mice
    ○ bluum
    ○ camp

15. ○ candle
    ○ clu
    ○ dish
    ○ evening

Name _____   Skill: Spelling—Test 8

DIRECTIONS:
Read each group of words. Mark the one that is **not** spelled correctly.

1. ○ folow
   ○ indoor
   ○ lesson
   ○ mile

2. ○ boddie
   ○ cannot
   ○ coin
   ○ doghouse

3. ○ forerest
   ○ half
   ○ invite
   ○ mind

4. ○ boss
   ○ card
   ○ cool
   ○ doun

5. ○ forgot
   ○ hang
   ○ lissen
   ○ mirror

6. ○ board
   ○ candy
   ○ dive
   ○ everbody

7. ○ foot
   ○ hair
   ○ interest
   ○ licke

8. ○ born
   ○ captin
   ○ cookie
   ○ dollar

9. ○ forget
   ○ hamer
   ○ itself
   ○ lift

10. ○ botle
    ○ carrot
    ○ corn
    ○ doorbell

11. ○ fool
    ○ instead
    ○ libary
    ○ milk

12. ○ boot
    ○ cap
    ○ collect
    ○ eskact

13. ○ forever
    ○ iland
    ○ life
    ○ mine

14. ○ both
    ○ carefull
    ○ copy
    ○ donkey

15. ○ happen
    ○ jarr
    ○ lock
    ○ moan

Name _____ Skill: Spelling—Test 9

DIRECTIONS:
Read each group of words. Mark the one that is **not** spelled correctly.

1. ○ bottem
   ○ carry
   ○ corner
   ○ doorway

2. ○ staje
   ○ pail
   ○ young
   ○ straw

3. ○ press
   ○ sandwich
   ○ sight
   ○ sentense

4. ○ ugly
   ○ spreed
   ○ travel
   ○ second

5. ○ vegtable
   ○ sense
   ○ sail
   ○ office

6. ○ nonne
   ○ pen
   ○ root
   ○ she'll

7. ○ sale
   ○ sholder
   ○ radio
   ○ plate

8. ○ third
   ○ slid
   ○ policce
   ○ return

9. ○ print
   ○ prinse
   ○ sack
   ○ purple

10. ○ strange
    ○ ritch
    ○ shade
    ○ rice

11. ○ vine
    ○ wunder
    ○ penny
    ○ north

12. ○ zoome
    ○ tape
    ○ quite
    ○ worry

13. ○ whole
    ○ sumer
    ○ safe
    ○ popcorn

14. ○ pony
    ○ slide
    ○ smart
    ○ wize

15. ○ unhappy
    ○ wave
    ○ quession
    ○ shut

Name _____   Skill: Synonyms—Test 1

DIRECTIONS:
Read each of the sentences below. Then, mark the word or phrase that means almost the same thing as the word or phrase that is underlined.

1. The <u>Earth</u> is round.

   ○ dirt
   ○ planet
   ○ eat

2. Those <u>women</u> are having a meeting.

   ○ men
   ○ children
   ○ ladies

3. I can't believe you ate <u>the whole</u> pie.

   ○ all of
   ○ none of
   ○ some of

4. Sue will <u>welcome</u> the guests at the door.

   ○ greet
   ○ say goodbye to
   ○ close

5. We had a <u>wonderful</u> time at the party.

   ○ great
   ○ awful
   ○ terrible

6. My father is a <u>wise</u> man.

   ○ old
   ○ smart
   ○ small

7. Gus can work <u>whenever</u> you need him.

   ○ today
   ○ never
   ○ any time

8. We will <u>go to see</u> my grandma at Thanksgiving.

   ○ wonder
   ○ worry
   ○ visit

© Carson-Dellosa CD-3734

Name _____ Skill: Synonyms—Test 2

DIRECTIONS:
Read each of the sentences below. Then, mark the word or phrase that means almost the same thing as the word or phrase that is underlined.

1. Can you <u>reach</u> the top shelf?
   - ○ travel
   - ○ ranch
   - ○ touch

2. Set your books <u>upon</u> the table.
   - ○ under
   - ○ over
   - ○ on top of

3. I <u>see</u> what you mean!
   - ○ understand
   - ○ don't get
   - ○ join

4. Please do not <u>tug</u> on my jacket.
   - ○ touch
   - ○ pull
   - ○ poke

5. I live in a small <u>village</u> near the ocean.
   - ○ house
   - ○ town
   - ○ country

6. Joe was <u>sad</u> when his puppy ran away.
   - ○ unhappy
   - ○ glad
   - ○ silly

7. Our muddy shoes made the floor look <u>ugly</u>.
   - ○ shiny
   - ○ brown
   - ○ not pretty

8. The policeman will <u>catch</u> the thief.
   - ○ trap
   - ○ see
   - ○ call to

Name _____   Skill: Synonyms—Test 5

DIRECTIONS:
Read each of the sentences below. Then, mark the word or phrase that means almost the same thing as the word or phrase that is underlined.

1. Sally will pull the sheets until they are <u>flat</u> on the bed.
   - ○ wrinkled
   - ○ smooth
   - ○ over

2. Put some <u>dirt</u> in the pot so we can plant the flower.
   - ○ soil
   - ○ seeds
   - ○ water

3. Please <u>rush</u> this letter to the postman.
   - ○ hurry
   - ○ mail
   - ○ ready

4. Will you <u>save</u> my place in line, please?
   - ○ keep
   - ○ give away
   - ○ stop

5. The dog stopped to <u>sniff</u> the trash can.
   - ○ bark at
   - ○ pull over
   - ○ smell

6. The skin on a toad feels <u>rough</u>.
   - ○ smooth
   - ○ bumpy
   - ○ hard

7. I will carry the doughnuts in a <u>sack</u>.
   - ○ paper
   - ○ pail
   - ○ bag

8. I did not mean to <u>frighten</u> you.
   - ○ fix
   - ○ scare
   - ○ stare at

Name _____   Skill: Synonyms—Test 6

DIRECTIONS:
Read each of the sentences below. Then, mark the word or phrase that means almost the same thing as the word or phrase that is underlined.

1. I will <u>seek</u> the answer to that question.
   - ○ forget
   - ○ give
   - ○ look for

2. I can <u>sense</u> that you are angry with me.
   - ○ feel
   - ○ sad
   - ○ look

3. I am <u>quick</u> with my math facts!
   - ○ fast
   - ○ smart
   - ○ slow

4. I must <u>return</u> my books to the library.
   - ○ borrow
   - ○ take back
   - ○ buy

5. Do not <u>yell</u> at your little sister!
   - ○ slap
   - ○ scream
   - ○ smile

6. I will <u>question</u> the man who saw what happened.
   - ○ listen to
   - ○ ask
   - ○ know

7. I need to <u>repair</u> my broken radio.
   - ○ throw away
   - ○ sell
   - ○ fix

8. Nan will <u>phone</u> us later today.
   - ○ shout
   - ○ call
   - ○ see

Name _____ Skill: Synonyms—Test 7

DIRECTIONS:
Read each of the sentences below. Then, mark the word or phrase that means almost the same thing as the word or phrase that is underlined.

1. Do you have a <u>present</u> for Bob?

   ○ gift
   ○ box
   ○ wrap

2. My frog can <u>jump</u> about three feet!

   ○ leap
   ○ slide
   ○ swim

3. The store is <u>nearby</u>.

   ○ away
   ○ far
   ○ close

4. Did you <u>pass</u> the red fence on the way here?

   ○ go by
   ○ hand over
   ○ climb

5. Did you <u>notice</u> that I got my hair cut?

   ○ see
   ○ like
   ○ feel

6. At the beginning of the race, Hal was <u>ahead</u>.

   ○ behind
   ○ in the lead
   ○ second

7. Put the flowers in the <u>center</u> of the table.

   ○ side
   ○ middle
   ○ back

8. Do not <u>peek</u> until I tell you!

   ○ talk
   ○ wake
   ○ look

Name _____ Skill: Synonyms—Test 8

DIRECTIONS:
Read each of the sentences below. Then, mark the word or phrase that means almost the same thing as the word or phrase that is underlined.

1. I will raise the window to let in fresh air.
   - ○ lift
   - ○ high
   - ○ under

2. Jim wants the blue ball instead of the red one.
   - ○ because
   - ○ as well as
   - ○ in place of

3. The book was hidden behind the chair.
   - ○ placed
   - ○ out of sight
   - ○ going

4. Bill made a giant pile of leaves when he raked.
   - ○ large
   - ○ loose
   - ○ small

5. I didn't listen to the music that was playing.
   - ○ talk
   - ○ hear
   - ○ earn

6. Will you invite Robert to your party?
   - ○ joke
   - ○ bring
   - ○ ask

7. The bears lived deep in the dark forest.
   - ○ woods
   - ○ mountains
   - ○ tree

8. The lights went out just as I entered the room.
   - ○ ran to
   - ○ went past
   - ○ went into

Name _____

Skill: Synonyms—Test 9

DIRECTIONS:
Read each of the sentences below. Then, mark the word or phrase that means almost the same thing as the word or phrase that is underlined.

1. I bent the tree branch too far and it <u>snapped</u>.

   ○ twisted
   ○ broke
   ○ grew

2. I have <u>a pair</u> of red shoes.

   ○ two
   ○ four
   ○ one

3. The class was <u>loud</u> while the teacher was gone.

   ○ quiet
   ○ wonderful
   ○ noisy

4. Sue was <u>certain</u> that the coat was hers.

   ○ happy
   ○ sure
   ○ right

5. I have one <u>cent</u> to put in my bank.

   ○ dollar
   ○ penny
   ○ dime

6. This dress is <u>perfect</u> for the party.

   ○ too small
   ○ colorful
   ○ just right

7. I must <u>hurry</u> or I will be late!

   ○ go fast
   ○ wait
   ○ hold

8. Put the <u>cover</u> on the pan so you don't get burned.

   ○ lid
   ○ lip
   ○ pot

© Carson-Dellosa CD-3734

Name _____   Skill: Antonyms—Test 1

DIRECTIONS:
Read each of the sentences below. Then, mark the word that means the opposite of the word that is underlined.

1. <u>Anyone</u> can come to the dance.
   - ○ no one
   - ○ everyone
   - ○ some

2. I was <u>asleep</u> at ten o'clock last night.
   - ○ rest
   - ○ awake
   - ○ eating

3. Do you have a swing in your <u>backyard</u>?
   - ○ front yard
   - ○ house
   - ○ yard

4. Put the old boxes in the <u>attic</u>.
   - ○ garage
   - ○ bedroom
   - ○ basement

5. Keep those two dogs <u>apart</u> or they will fight.
   - ○ over
   - ○ away
   - ○ together

6. My <u>aunt</u> gave me a bike for my birthday.
   - ○ lady
   - ○ grandmother
   - ○ uncle

7. The family in the story was very <u>poor</u>.
   - ○ nice
   - ○ rich
   - ○ mean

8. I will read a book <u>after</u> I take a bath.
   - ○ while
   - ○ before
   - ○ soon

© Carson-Dellosa CD-3734

Name _____   Skill: Antonyms—Test 2

DIRECTIONS:
Read each of the sentences below. Then, mark the word that means the opposite of the word that is underlined.

1. Janice was <u>behind</u> Ted in the lunch line.
   - ○ beside
   - ○ next to
   - ○ ahead of

2. Do you want to <u>add</u> anything to the drawing?
   - ○ give
   - ○ take away
   - ○ say

3. Will you vote <u>for</u> John as class president?
   - ○ with
   - ○ against
   - ○ open

4. I was so <u>happy</u> when I heard the news.
   - ○ pleased
   - ○ sad
   - ○ silly

5. Put your hat on the shelf <u>above</u> the coats.
   - ○ below
   - ○ over
   - ○ behind

6. There are times when I am very <u>brave</u>.
   - ○ afraid
   - ○ bold
   - ○ mean

7. We are <u>alike</u> in many ways!
   - ○ different
   - ○ the same
   - ○ friends

8. Wrap the present in <u>plain</u> paper.
   - ○ white
   - ○ flat
   - ○ fancy

Name _____   Skill: Antonyms—Test 3

DIRECTIONS:
Read each of the sentences below. Then, mark the word that means the opposite of the word that is underlined.

1. <u>Both</u> of us were glad to get home.

   ○ neither
   ○ two
   ○ all

2. Judy <u>bought</u> six toys at the yard sale.

   ○ sold
   ○ gave
   ○ had

3. Did you <u>break</u> the glass in the window?

   ○ crack
   ○ fix
   ○ glue

4. Bring water <u>to</u> the picnic.

   ○ from
   ○ on
   ○ when

5. Is this the <u>bottom</u> of the box?

   ○ end
   ○ side
   ○ top

6. I was very <u>brave</u> when the cat jumped out at me.

   ○ nice
   ○ happy
   ○ scared

7. I found a <u>bright</u> penny in the grass.

   ○ dull
   ○ new
   ○ shiny

8. This is a <u>short</u> story.

   ○ good
   ○ long
   ○ small

Name _____   Skill: Antonyms—Test 4

DIRECTIONS:
Read each of the sentences below. Then, mark the word that means the opposite of the word that is underlined.

1. I <u>gave</u> a present.

   ○ have
   ○ see
   ○ took

2. Will your dad <u>buy</u> that car?

   ○ paint
   ○ drive
   ○ sell

3. Tim was <u>careful</u> with the glass plate.

   ○ safe
   ○ careless
   ○ hungry

4. I was <u>certain</u> I left the book on the table!

   ○ easy
   ○ not sure
   ○ told

5. Jill has <u>a few</u> holes in her socks.

   ○ two
   ○ some
   ○ many

6. I <u>cannot</u> go to the movie with you.

   ○ doesn't
   ○ will
   ○ won't

7. Did you <u>catch</u> the ball?

   ○ drop
   ○ hold
   ○ hit

8. The crowd began to <u>cheer</u> for the team.

   ○ laugh
   ○ yell for
   ○ boo

Name _____   Skill: Antonyms—Test 5

DIRECTIONS:
Read each of the sentences below. Then, mark the word that means the opposite of the word that is underlined.

---

1. The fox was very <u>clever</u> in this story!

   ○ dumb
   ○ smart
   ○ fluffy

2. It is a little <u>warm</u> outside today.

   ○ rainy
   ○ hot
   ○ cool

3. Julie was <u>angry</u> because she lost her boot.

   ○ happy
   ○ sad
   ○ tired

4. We will set up the tent in the <u>daytime</u>.

   ○ shade
   ○ noon
   ○ night time

5. Will you <u>collect</u> the lunch money now?

   ○ pick up
   ○ give out
   ○ pack

6. I had to <u>crawl</u> across the room.

   ○ walk
   ○ look
   ○ creep

7. My <u>daughter</u> goes to your school.

   ○ child
   ○ son
   ○ sister

8. Please <u>shut</u> the door as you leave the room.

   ○ close
   ○ open
   ○ slam

Name _____   Skill: Antonyms—Test 6

DIRECTIONS:
Read each of the sentences below. Then, mark the word that means the opposite of the word that is underlined.

1. Feed the plant a lot if you want it to <u>live</u>.

   ○ die
   ○ grow
   ○ turn green

2. Will you <u>fill</u> a big hole for me?

   ○ dirt
   ○ dig
   ○ jump in

3. After the big storm, I was <u>dry</u>!

   ○ hot
   ○ cold
   ○ wet

4. Is that glass <u>empty</u>?

   ○ broken
   ○ full
   ○ ugly

5. Would you like a seat that is <u>different</u>?

   ○ not the same
   ○ higher
   ○ the same

6. Do not <u>drop</u> the baby!

   ○ play with
   ○ lift
   ○ sit on

7. Please don't come to my house too <u>early</u>.

   ○ late
   ○ soon
   ○ quick

8. That boy is my <u>friend</u>.

   ○ cousin
   ○ pal
   ○ enemy

© Carson-Dellosa CD-3734

Name _____   Skill: Antonyms—Test 7

DIRECTIONS:
Read each of the sentences below. Then, mark the word that means the opposite of the word that is underlined.

1. Can you get any <u>closer</u>?

   ○ nearer
   ○ farther
   ○ front

2. This is the <u>first</u> time I will write this story.

   ○ final
   ○ second
   ○ almost

3. Will this ball <u>float</u> in the water?

   ○ play
   ○ bounce
   ○ sink

4. Can you <u>remember</u> this short story?

   ○ forget
   ○ write
   ○ repeat

5. That clown is very <u>fat</u>!

   ○ puffy
   ○ fluffy
   ○ thin

6. Cross this line to <u>start</u> the race.

   ○ finish
   ○ begin
   ○ win

7. Get in line and you can <u>follow</u> us.

   ○ get behind
   ○ lead
   ○ play with

8. Get to the <u>back</u> of the line!

   ○ side
   ○ front
   ○ end

Name _____   Skill: Antonyms—Test 8

DIRECTIONS:
Read each of the sentences below. Then, mark the word that means the opposite of the word that is underlined.

1. That is a <u>giant</u> teddy bear!

   ● big
   ○ funny
   ○ tiny

2. This was a very <u>hard</u> test!

   ○ different
   ○ easy
   ○ bad

3. The book seemed <u>heavy</u> when I carried it.

   ○ light
   ○ hard
   ○ easy

4. We must be <u>quiet</u> in this room.

   ○ happy
   ○ good
   ○ loud

5. We <u>happily</u> went to the store for mother.

   ○ joyfully
   ○ smilingly
   ○ sadly

6. I <u>love</u> to eat pickles with peanut butter.

   ○ hate
   ○ enjoy
   ○ don't

7. A <u>huge</u> moth landed on the tree.

   ○ fuzzy
   ○ small
   ○ big

8. The birds flew <u>south</u> this morning.

   ○ east
   ○ north
   ○ away

Name _____   Skill: Antonyms—Test 9

DIRECTIONS:
Read each of the sentences below. Then, mark the word that means the opposite of the word that is underlined.

1. The windows in the old house were <u>bare</u>.

   ○ covered
   ○ empty
   ○ dark

2. Has that camera been <u>broken</u> for very long?

   ○ fixed
   ○ not working
   ○ used

3. Is the <u>moon</u> in the sky yet?

   ○ sun
   ○ star
   ○ airplane

4. I have a <u>question</u> for you!

   ○ problem
   ○ mess
   ○ answer

5. Brian painted a picture of a day in <u>winter</u>.

   ○ fall
   ○ summer
   ○ snow

6. It is very <u>cloudy</u> outside today.

   ○ not right
   ○ furry
   ○ sunny

7. The <u>child</u> wanted to play with us.

   ○ baby
   ○ adult
   ○ boy

8. Andy likes to <u>share</u> all his cookies.

   ○ give away
   ○ keep
   ○ eat

Name _____   Skill: Vocabulary—Test 1

DIRECTIONS:
Choose the word that best completes each sentence. Mark the correct word.

1. To be able to do something means you _____.
   - ○ like to start things
   - ○ are not ready
   - ○ can do it

2. To add numbers you _____.
   - ○ take them apart
   - ○ put them together
   - ○ put them into groups

3. If I put the lamp against the wall it is _____ the wall.
   - ○ far away
   - ○ next to
   - ○ on top of

4. The word also means _____.
   - ○ after
   - ○ without
   - ○ too

5. When something is above your head it is _____ you.
   - ○ under
   - ○ over
   - ○ beneath

6. To be afraid is to be _____.
   - ○ scared
   - ○ angry
   - ○ very happy

7. John is ahead in the race. He is _____.
   - ○ last
   - ○ behind someone
   - ○ in front

8. When I get really mad I am _____.
   - ○ angry
   - ○ hot
   - ○ shy

Name _____   Skill: Vocabulary—Test 2

DIRECTIONS:
Choose the word that best completes each sentence. Mark the correct word.

1. A word that means not together is _____.
   ○ with
   ○ apart
   ○ next to

2. I want to catch a mouse, so I will _____.
   ○ watch it
   ○ play with it
   ○ set a trap for it

3. If my glass is empty, then it has _____.
   ○ something in it
   ○ a lot in it
   ○ nothing in it

4. If a test is really hard, then it is _____.
   ○ easy
   ○ difficult
   ○ fun

5. Another word for under is _____.
   ○ below
   ○ on
   ○ beside

6. To collect fire wood is to _____ it.
   ○ gather
   ○ match
   ○ trade

7. If Jan follows me in her car, then she will _____.
   ○ go in front of me
   ○ come behind me
   ○ not go at all

8. To have a job means you have to _____.
   ○ work
   ○ go home
   ○ play

Name _____   Skill: Vocabulary—Test 3

DIRECTIONS:
Choose the word that best completes each sentence. Mark the correct word.

1. A market is another word for a _____.
   - ○ playground
   - ○ school
   - ○ store

2. Do not peek means the same as do not _____.
   - ○ talk
   - ○ look
   - ○ move

3. I fell asleep on the way home, so I was _____.
   - ○ gone
   - ○ awake
   - ○ not awake

4. A word that means many cows is _____.
   - ○ cattle
   - ○ mice
   - ○ cow

5. An ocean is a large _____.
   - ○ body of water
   - ○ airplane
   - ○ building

6. A word that means to take something back is _____.
   - ○ return
   - ○ borrow
   - ○ give

7. A word that means next to is _____.
   - ○ away
   - ○ below
   - ○ beside

8. If Mary is upset today, then she is ____.
   - ○ sad
   - ○ pretty
   - ○ glad

© Carson-Dellosa CD-3734

Name _____   Skill: Vocabulary—Test 4

DIRECTIONS:
Choose the word that best completes each sentence. Mark the correct word.

---

1. To enter a room means that you will _____.
   - ○ leave
   - ○ go in
   - ○ paint it

2. Work done after school is called _____.
   - ○ play
   - ○ homework
   - ○ stuff

3. Another word for message is _____.
   - ○ note
   - ○ rub
   - ○ eat

4. To make something perfect is to make it _____.
   - ○ right
   - ○ wrong
   - ○ ugly

5. I will always remember you. Always means _____.
   - ○ for three years
   - ○ never
   - ○ forever

6. The word join means to _____.
   - ○ take apart
   - ○ bring together
   - ○ joke

7. An office is a place where people _____.
   - ○ grow plants
   - ○ live
   - ○ work

8. A robber is a _____.
   - ○ friend
   - ○ good person
   - ○ thief

Name _____   Skill: Vocabulary—Test 9

DIRECTIONS:
Choose the word that best completes each sentence. Mark the correct word.

1. I own four pets. To own means _____.
   - ○ to feed
   - ○ to have
   - ○ to give

2. To scold someone is to _____.
   - ○ burn them
   - ○ yell at them
   - ○ be nice to them

3. A fact is something that is _____.
   - ○ true
   - ○ not true
   - ○ unreal

4. To track an animal is to _____.
   - ○ scare
   - ○ follow
   - ○ look at

5. The word probably means _____.
   - ○ not really
   - ○ likely
   - ○ maybe not

6. When I am not wet, I am _____.
   - ○ dry
   - ○ damp
   - ○ cold

7. Something that is golden is _____.
   - ○ brown
   - ○ round
   - ○ bright yellow

8. A word that means to get together is _____.
   - ○ shop
   - ○ miss
   - ○ meet

Name _____   Skill: Vocabulary—Test 10

DIRECTIONS:
Choose the word that best completes each sentence. Mark the correct word.

1. If I beat you in a race, I _____.
   ○ quit
   ○ win
   ○ lose

2. When you are early you are _____.
   ○ on time
   ○ late
   ○ ahead of time

3. A person that is clever is _____.
   ○ smart
   ○ dumb
   ○ sick

4. A word that means not many is _____.
   ○ plenty
   ○ lot
   ○ few

5. A breeze is a _____.
   ○ small bee
   ○ big cloud
   ○ small wind

6. To build is to _____.
   ○ make
   ○ take down
   ○ go in

7. Another word for world is _____.
   ○ map
   ○ earth
   ○ state

8. My mom's dad is my _____.
   ○ uncle
   ○ cousin
   ○ grandpa

Name _____   Skill: Vocabulary—Test 11

DIRECTIONS:
Choose the word that best completes each sentence. Mark the correct word.

1. An idea is a _____.

   ○ thought
   ○ friend
   ○ kind of game

2. A small part of an hour is _____.

   ○ a day
   ○ mine
   ○ a minute

3. The foot of a dog is called the _____.

   ○ tail
   ○ paw
   ○ hoof

4. Another name for a heavy blanket is a _____.

   ○ quilt
   ○ pillow
   ○ sheet

5. If something is loose it is _____.

   ○ gone
   ○ not tight
   ○ small

6. Something that comes in a set of two is a _____.

   ○ pair
   ○ part
   ○ point

7. To show that something is right is to _____.

   ○ pick
   ○ show
   ○ prove

8. A group of words that go together is a _____.

   ○ word
   ○ sentence
   ○ puzzle

© Carson-Dellosa CD-3734

Name _____   Skill: Vocabulary—Test 12

DIRECTIONS:
Choose the word that best completes each sentence. Mark the correct word.

1. I go before you so I am _____.
   - ○ last
   - ○ in front
   - ○ behind

2. To climb a tree is to _____.
   - ○ go up
   - ○ get down
   - ○ build in

3. A word that means to cut in two is _____.
   - ○ part
   - ○ chop
   - ○ halve

4. A sneaker is a kind of _____.
   - ○ pet
   - ○ game
   - ○ shoe

5. Another word for cap is _____.
   - ○ boy
   - ○ raincoat
   - ○ hat

6. To be at the end of a line is to be _____.
   - ○ first
   - ○ middle
   - ○ last

7. Another word for invite is _____.
   - ○ put together
   - ○ ask
   - ○ tell

8. When something is terrible it is very _____.
   - ○ sweet
   - ○ nice
   - ○ awful

Name _____   Skill: Vocabulary—Test 13

DIRECTIONS:
Choose the word that best completes each sentence. Mark the correct word.

1. To zoom means to _____.
   ○ move quickly
   ○ move slowly
   ○ go by train

2. To close just one eye is to _____.
   ○ stink
   ○ blink
   ○ wink

3. To know what something means is to _____.
   ○ not get
   ○ understand
   ○ hold

4. The word taste means _____.
   ○ to feel
   ○ to wait for
   ○ to take a bite

5. A person who is smart is _____.
   ○ worn
   ○ wise
   ○ not bright

6. A word that means to feel is _____.
   ○ touch
   ○ tap
   ○ skin

7. The woman a man marries becomes his _____.
   ○ neighbor
   ○ daughter
   ○ wife

8. Another word for twig is _____.
   ○ branch
   ○ bunch
   ○ tree

Name _____ Skill: Reading Sentences

DIRECTIONS:
Read each of the sentences below. Use the picture to help decide which word best completes the story. Mark the space for each answer you choose.

We made a tent in my back yard. We used an old

1. blink   blanket   jacket
   ○   ○   ○

and some rope. We tied the rope

2. beside   over   between
   ○   ○   ○

two trees and hung the blanket on it. That night we

3. swam   camped   cramp
   ○   ○   ○

in the tent. It was close to the house so we were not

4. scared.   angry.   glad.
   ○   ○   ○

George went skiing with his father. He wore a hat and

1. scarf   skate   spin
   ○   ○   ○

because it was cold. First, they went to the top of a

2. hall.   mountain.   month.
   ○   ○   ○

George did not know how to ski so he had to take

3. lessons.   markets.   before.
   ○   ○   ○

Then he and his dad went all the way to the

4. behind.   bottom.   moon.
   ○   ○   ○

Name _____

Skill: Reading Sentences

DIRECTIONS:
Read each of the sentences below. Use the picture to help decide which word best completes the story. Mark the space for each answer you choose.

Each fall we pick apples. My brother and I

1. cross   clip   climb
   ○   ○   ○

up the tree to find the biggest apples. Mother has a

2. **ladder**   letter   listen
   ○   ○   ○

because she can't reach high

3. **edge.**   enough.   kept.
   ○   ○   ○

We pick so many apples we can make six

4. **throws!**   plates!   pies!
   ○   ○   ○

Sam took a test today. The test was on his

1. shake   spelling   soft
   ○   ○   ○

words. Some of the words were

2. quick   whisper   difficult
   ○   ○   ○

to spell. Sam did not

3. study   past   peek
   ○   ○   ○

well last night. He was surprised at his poor

4. drop.   grade.   grab.
   ○   ○   ○

Name _____   Skill: Reading Sentences

DIRECTIONS:
Read each of the sentences below. Use the picture to help decide which word best completes the story. Mark the space for each answer you choose.

I am a tall animal. I am tall because I have a long

1. **head.**   **neck.**   **nine.**
   ○   ○   ○

When I want water, I have to bend my

2. **tail**   **knees**   **knew**
   ○   ○   ○

to reach the ground. I think that I am

3. **lucky**   **lift**   **neither**
   ○   ○   ○

to be so tall. Many of my friends are much too

4. **print.**   **shade.**   **short.**
   ○   ○   ○

I really like to play outside. Best of all, I like to

1. **notice.**   **silver.**   **skate.**
   ○   ○   ○

I roll down my sidewalk and out into the

2. **street.**   **ship.**   **smoke.**
   ○   ○   ○

I go very quickly and then stop and

3. **splash**   **spin**   **speak**
   ○   ○   ○

around. In every race, I am always the

4. **winner.**   **wander.**   **twig.**
   ○   ○   ○

© Carson-Dellosa CD-3734

Name _____   Skill: Reading Sentences

DIRECTIONS:
Read each of the sentences below. Use the picture to help decide which word best completes the story. Mark the space for each answer you choose.

Polly is my pet bird. She is a blue and green

1. painter.   parrot.   path.
   ○   ○   ○

Polly talks a lot. She can

2. rest   remember   rail
   ○   ○   ○

many words that she has

3. locked.   left.   learned.
   ○   ○   ○

All of my friends think that Polly is

4. wire.   wonderful.   wheel.
   ○   ○   ○

It was a dark night in the woods. I was a little

1. afraid   alike   belong
   ○   ○   ○

because I did not have a light and the

2. mask   moon   junk
   ○   ○   ○

was behind a cloud. Suddenly I heard a loud

3. noise!   notice!   pole!
   ○   ○   ○

I looked up and saw that it was only a baby

4. quack.   office.   owl.
   ○   ○   ○

© Carson-Dellosa CD-3734   68

Name _____   Skill: Reading Sentences

DIRECTIONS:
Read each of the sentences below. Use the picture to help decide which word best completes the story. Mark the space for each answer you choose.

Once there was a king and queen. They lived in a big

1. **circle**   **chase**   **castle**
   ○   ○   ○

near the sea. They had a son who was a good

2. **mark.**   **price.**   **prince.**
   ○   ○   ○

One day he rode to another castle and saw a beautiful

3. **young**   **year**   **teach**
   ○   ○   ○

girl. They fell in love and got

4. **met.**   **married.**   **mail.**
   ○   ○   ○

I saw a horse today. It was

1. **dive**   **different**   **done**
   ○   ○   ○

from any horse I had ever seen! It had black and white

2. **salt!**   **slides!**   **stripes!**
   ○   ○   ○

I had never seen such a

3. **shape**   **sense**   **strange**
   ○   ○   ○

horse before. Maybe it was really just a silly

4. **drew.**   **dream.**   **drum.**
   ○   ○   ○

© Carson-Dellosa CD-3734

Name _____

Skill: Reading Sentences

DIRECTIONS:
Read each of the sentences below. Use the picture to help decide which word best completes the story. Mark the space for each answer you choose.

This is my town. It is a good place to

1. **live.**   life.   key.
   ○   ○   ○

My town has a bank and many stores. We have one

2. **front**   factory   flour
   ○   ○   ○

where many people work. The farmers grow corn and

3. **cattle.**   land.   hidden.
   ○   ○   ○

Nurses and doctors work at our

4. **Monday.**   hospital.   happen.
   ○   ○   ○

Kyle likes art. He likes to draw and make

1. **whole.**   paintings.   mud.
   ○   ○   ○

He takes his time and will never

2. **rush**   rough   shine
   ○   ○   ○

when he paints. He puts different colors on a

3. **pass**   palette   potato
   ○   ○   ○

and mixes them together. Kyle is a very good

4. **baby.**   agree.   artist.
   ○   ○   ○

© Carson-Dellosa CD-3734

Name _____   Skill: Reading Sentences

DIRECTIONS:
Read each of the sentences below. Use the picture to help decide which word best completes the story. Mark the space for each answer you choose.

Amy likes school. Her favorite class is

1. **music.**   mirror.   learn.
   ○   ○   ○

Amy can play a

2. **five**   fair   few
   ○   ○   ○

songs on her

3. **violin.**   vine.   voice.
   ○   ○   ○

But sometimes she breaks a

4. **string!**   wing!   spent!
   ○   ○   ○

I like when it begins to rain. The

1. child   **clouds**   curl
   ○   ○   ○

gather and it begins to

2. spend.   stood.   **storm.**
   ○   ○   ○

I like to hear the rain and the loud

3. taste.   **thunder.**   toast.
   ○   ○   ○

When it is over, I can always find the

4. for.   **rainbow.**   flower.
   ○   ○   ○

© Carson-Dellosa CD-3734   71

Name _____   Skill: Reading Sentences

DIRECTIONS:
Read each of the sentences below. Use the picture to help decide which word best completes the story. Mark the space for each answer you choose.

I like to watch bees. I am

1. catch   careful   cherry
    ○   ○   ○

when I am near them because they can

2. sting.   stare.   reach.
    ○   ○   ○

They live in a large

3. hive.   horn.   gate.
    ○   ○   ○

That is where they make lots of

4. held.   honey.   hair.
    ○   ○   ○

Lots of animals live in the woods. This one is a

1. player.   owl.   raccoon.
    ○   ○   ○

It is a dark color and has a lot of rings on its

2. tail.   trail.   touch.
    ○   ○   ○

Every raccoon has a

3. march   mask   main
    ○   ○   ○

around its eyes that makes it look like a

4. river.   robber.   roller.
    ○   ○   ○

© Carson-Dellosa CD-3734

Name _____   Skill: Reading Sentences

DIRECTIONS:
Read each of the sentences below. Use the picture to help decide which word best completes the story. Mark the space for each answer you choose.

Jamie has a pet rabbit. Some people call it a

1. **bunny.**   honey.   knot.
   ○   ○   ○

Jamie must see that the rabbit gets enough food and

2. **drop**   except   exercise
   ○   ○   ○

so it does not get sick. It likes to eat

3. **carrots**   coins   cattle
   ○   ○   ○

and other

4. **paw.**   vegetables.   visit.
   ○   ○   ○

Pam is so happy! She is going to the

1. circle   gate   **circus**
   ○   ○   ○

this week. Some men put up a big

2. **tent**   team   thumb
   ○   ○   ○

and brought in lots of

3. worry   **wonderful**   whole
   ○   ○   ○

animals. The circus will even have a

4. pipe!   **parade!**   patch!
   ○   ○   ○

© Carson-Dellosa CD-3734

Name _____   Skill: Narrative Passages

DIRECTIONS:
Read each story. Then, read each question and mark the space for the answer you think is right. Write your answer for number five on a separate sheet of paper.

Sometimes it is best to be slow. When you are doing work that needs to be done carefully, you should take your time. Being the fastest is not always being the best!

1. The story is about being

   best ○   slow ○   quick ○

2. Fast is not always

   time ○   bad ○   best ○

3. Go slow when you must be

   careful ○   quick ○   first ○

4. A good name for this story might be
   - ○ **Faster is Better**
   - ○ **Slow and Careful**
   - ○ **The Slow Snail**

5. Name a job or time when you need to be slow.

Mom just had a new baby. I do not have any fun with him. He sleeps all day and can't play yet. Mom spends a lot of time with him.

1. Mom had a

   girl ○   nap ○   baby ○

2. What does he do all day?

   play ○   eat ○   sleep ○

3. The new baby is my

   brother ○   sister ○   pal ○

4. How do I feel about the baby?
   - ○ **I don't like him much**
   - ○ **I like to hold him**
   - ○ **We are good friends**

5. How might I change my feelings about the baby?

Name _____

Skill: Narrative Passages

DIRECTIONS:
Read each story. Then, read each question and mark the space for the answer you think is right. Write your answer for number five on a separate sheet of paper.

There is a treehouse in the back yard. Do you want to play there? It has a rope to swing from. We can pretend to be anything we like. No one will find us up there.

1. I want to play in a

   tree **treehouse** **yard**
   ○　　　○　　　○

2. What is in the treehouse?

   a chair **a rope** **a swing**
   ○　　　○　　　○

3. Why do I like the treehouse?

   it is tall **it is scary** **it is fun**
   ○　　　○　　　○

4. Why won't anyone find us up there?
   ○ **everyone is sleeping**
   ○ **the leaves hide us**
   ○ **we are invisible**

5. What games would you play in a treehouse?

Alyssa takes dancing lessons. She has learned to move and spin with the music. She listens carefully and does what the teacher says. Alyssa would like to be a dancer when she grows up.

1. Who is the girl in the story?

   Mary **teacher** **Alyssa**
   ○　　　○　　　○

2. She learns by taking

   lessons **music** **dancer**
   ○　　　○　　　○

3. Alyssa _____ dancing.

   hates **enjoys** **stopped**
   ○　　　○　　　○

4. What tells you how Alyssa feels about dancing? She
   ○ **learned to spin**
   ○ **takes lessons**
   ○ **wants to be a dancer**

5. What kind of dance do you think Alyssa is learning?

© Carson-Dellosa CD-3734

Name _____   Skill: Narrative Passages

DIRECTIONS:
Read each story. Then, read each question and mark the space for the answer you think is right. Write your answer for number five on a separate sheet of paper.

Roger has a rock collection. He takes long walks in the mountains and picks up rocks that he sees. Some rocks are as big as a box. Others are so tiny you can hardly see them!

1. Who collects rocks?

   Roger　　**boxes**　　**Father**
   　○　　　　　○　　　　　○

2. He found his rocks in the

   ocean　　**mountains**　　**sand**
   　○　　　　　○　　　　　○

3. Roger must like to

   run　　**walk**　　**eat**
   　○　　　○　　　○

4. Roger looks for rocks in the mountains because
   ○ **he likes to climb**
   ○ **many rocks are there**
   ○ **it is cooler**

5. What is an easy thing to collect? Why?

It is the time of year when the pond is starting to burst with life. Fish are laying eggs. Butterflies are on all the flowers. The water is fresh and clear. Frogs croak and sing all night.

1. What croaks at night?

   frogs　　**flowers**　　**fish**
   　○　　　　　○　　　　　○

2. What are laying eggs?

   frogs　　**butterflies**　　**fish**
   　○　　　　　○　　　　　○

3. Life at the pond is

   lonely　　**ugly**　　**happy**
   　○　　　　　○　　　　　○

4. What time of year is it?
   ○ **fall**
   ○ **winter**
   ○ **spring**

5. What is your favorite time of year? Why?

Name _____   Skill: Narrative Passages

DIRECTIONS:
Read each story. Then, read each question and mark the space for the answer you think is right. Write your answer for number five on a separate sheet of paper.

David has a box of magic tricks. He does tricks for his friends. David wears a tall hat and black cape. He waves a wand and pulls a rabbit from his hat. His friends ask him to do it again.

1. David wears a black

   hat   cape   wand
   ○   ○   ○

2. What comes from the hat?

   rabbit   magic   wand
   ○   ○   ○

3. David wants to be a

   student   magician   friend
   ○   ○   ○

4. What do David's friends think about his trick?
   ○ they don't care
   ○ they really like it
   ○ they are scared

5. Which is better, the rabbit trick or a disappearing coin?

I went to the store with Dad. I stopped to look at a great toy. When I looked up, Dad was gone. He was lost! I was a little scared so I called his name. Dad came around the corner and smiled.

1. We were at the

   school   store   bank
   ○   ○   ○

2. What made me stop?

   Dad   a toy   a man
   ○   ○   ○

3. Who was really lost?

   Dad   me   you
   ○   ○   ○

4. Why was Dad gone?
   ○ he went to get eat lunch
   ○ he stopped to look
   ○ he didn't know I stopped

5. Who was lost, Dad or me? Why?

Name _____

Skill: Narrative Passages

DIRECTIONS:
Read each story. Then, read each question and mark the space for the answer you think is right. Write your answer for number five on a separate sheet of paper.

There is a new girl at my school. Her name is Nancy, and she smiles a lot. She sits behind me but doesn't say much. I wonder what she likes to do for fun. Maybe I will ask her to play with me.

1. The new girl's name is

   Mimi   Natalie   Nancy
   ○   ○   ○

2. She sits _____ me.

   next to   behind   beside
   ○   ○   ○

3. Nancy is probably

   mean   shy   angry
   ○   ○   ○

4. Nancy is probably quiet because she
   - ○ is a little scared
   - ○ doesn't like children
   - ○ wants to eat lunch

5. What can you do to help a new student at school?

I ate an apple and put the seeds in a cup. I put water on the seeds and left them alone for one week. I put the seeds into a pot of dirt. With lots of water and sun, it might grow!

1. What did I eat?

   pear   peach   apple
   ○   ○   ○

2. First, I put the seeds in

   a cup   water   dirt
   ○   ○   ○

3. I left the seeds in water for

   3 days   7 days   8 days
   ○   ○   ○

4. If the seeds grow, they will become
   - ○ a giant tree
   - ○ an oak tree
   - ○ an apple tree

5. What is the best kind of plant to grow indoors?

Name _____

Skill: Narrative Passages

DIRECTIONS:
Read each story. Then, read each question and mark the space for the answer you think is right. Write your answer for number five on a separate sheet of paper.

Mother says I have to shine my shoes. They are dusty and have a little mud on the bottom. Mother says I cannot go if my shoes are dirty. I like them just the way they are.

1. My shoes are

   old   dusty   smelly
   ○   ○   ○

2. If I don't shine them I can't

   eat   run   go
   ○   ○   ○

3. My shoes do not look

   clean   used   black
   ○   ○   ○

4. Mother wants them to look nice because
   ○ she likes dirty shoes
   ○ she wants new shoes
   ○ they will look better

5. Do you think I should shine my shoes? Why?

It was a day in July. James had been playing in the yard. He wanted something cold to drink. He got the hose and turned it on. Splash! Water hit him right in the face!

1. What was James doing?

   skating   running   playing
   ○   ○   ○

2. James wanted a cold

   hose   drink   day
   ○   ○   ○

3. It was probably a ___ day.

   cool   hot   rainy
   ○   ○   ○

4. How did James feel? He was probably
   ○ angry at the hose
   ○ happy to cool off
   ○ sad to waste water

5. What should James do now that he is so wet?

Name _____

Skill: Narrative Passages

DIRECTIONS:
Read each story. Then, read each question and mark the space for the answer you think is right. Write your answer for number five on a separate sheet of paper.

Today has been a terrible day. I banged my knee on the bed. I lost one of my good shoes and had to wear an old pair. In the spelling bee, I lost right away. What else can go wrong?

1. What kind of day was it?

    terrible   wonderful   nice
       ○   ○   ○

2. I hurt my

    shoe   head   knee
     ○   ○   ○

3. How do I feel about today?

    happy   excited   angry
      ○   ○   ○

4. Where did this story take place?
    ○ in the backyard
    ○ at home and school
    ○ at the store

5. What can I do to make it a better day?

Ted is a taxi. He picks up people and takes them to different places. He likes his job. He gets to meet many nice people. He gets to see everything in the city. Ted is a happy taxi.

1. The taxi's name is

    Joe   people   Ted
     ○   ○   ○

2. The taxi takes people

    to work   home   places
       ○   ○   ○

3. Ted cannot go

    in rivers   home   to work
       ○   ○   ○

4. Ted likes his job because he
    ○ likes to see things
    ○ hates to travel
    ○ wants to be a person

5. What makes a job good?

© Carson-Dellosa CD-3734

Name _____   Skill: Expository Passages

DIRECTIONS:
Read each story. Then, read each question or statement and mark the space for the answer you think is right. Write your answer for number five on a separate sheet of paper.

People live together in towns or cities. They help each other by the jobs they do. A place where people live and work together is called a community.

1. People help each other by having different
   - **towns** ○
   - **jobs** ○
   - **cities** ○

2. A town or city is where people live and work
   - **together** ○
   - **for fun** ○
   - **apart** ○

3. Which place is not a community for people?
   - **town** ○
   - **village** ○
   - **river** ○

4. People help each other because we cannot
   - ○ **do everything alone**
   - ○ **have friends**
   - ○ **live alone**

5. What jobs do you think help people the most?

Police officers are people who help in your community. Their job is to see that people obey the laws that keep us safe. Police watch over our roads, neighborhoods and stores.

1. Who watches over our community?
   - **police** ○
   - **laws** ○
   - **stores** ○

2. Police officers make sure all people obey our
   - **job** ○
   - **roads** ○
   - **laws** ○

3. It is good to have police around because they
   - **laugh a lot** ○
   - **protect us** ○
   - **are cute** ○

4. The police are people that
   - ○ **chase us**
   - ○ **help a community**
   - ○ **put out fires**

5. Why do the police give tickets for speeding?

© Carson-Dellosa CD-3734

Name _____   Skill: Expository Passages

DIRECTIONS:
Read each story. Then, read each question or statement and mark the space for the answer you think is right. Write your answer for number five on a separate sheet of paper.

Who helps when a building catches on fire? Firefighters do. They bring large trucks with long hoses. They go into burning homes to save people who are still inside. They fight fires with water.

1. Who puts out fires?

police	teachers	firefighters
○	○	○

2. What is used to put out fires?

trucks	ladders	water
○	○	○

3. A firefighter's job is

easy	fun	dangerous
○	○	○

4. Firefighters help keep us

   ○ from getting sick
   ○ safe
   ○ from breaking laws

5. Would you like to be a firefighter? Why or why not?

Doctors are people who help others. We go to a doctor when we are sick or hurt. Doctors find what is wrong and give us medicine or fix broken bones. We need doctors in our community.

1. Doctors can help us when we are

sick	tired	old
○	○	○

2. A doctor might give us

a cold	medicine	a bone
○	○	○

3. Doctors can also help keep us

young	rich	healthy
○	○	○

4. You would go to a doctor if you

   ○ had a broken TV
   ○ ate dinner
   ○ broke your leg

5. What does your doctor do to help you?

Name _____

Skill: Expository Passages

DIRECTIONS:
Read each story. Then, read each question or statement and mark the space for the answer you think is right. Write your answer for number five on a separate sheet of paper.

When you have a sore tooth you go to a dentist. Dentists live in our community. They help keep our teeth clean and healthy. They can fix a chipped tooth or fill a cavity.

1. What is this story about?

   dentists   **teeth**   **cleaning**
   ○   ○   ○

2. Dentists help us keep our teeth

   chipped   **healthy**   **sore**
   ○   ○   ○

3. A dentist helps us take care of our

   hair   **body**   **mouth**
   ○   ○   ○

4. A dentist can
   ○ fix a broken arm
   ○ fill a cavity
   ○ give out speeding tickets

5. Describe what it is like when you visit the dentist.

Farmers are part of our community. They grow many of the foods we eat. Farmers raise animals that are used for food and clothing. We need farmers so we have good things to eat.

1. Farmers help communities by growing

   cows   **tomatoes**   **food**
   ○   ○   ○

2. Animals can be used for clothing and

   pets   **food**   **jobs**
   ○   ○   ○

3. Without farmers, many people would be

   hungry   **old**   **fat**
   ○   ○   ○

4. Farmers are a part of our
   ○ cars
   ○ communities
   ○ corn

5. How did a farmer help you today?

© Carson-Dellosa CD-3734

Name _____   Skill: Expository Passages

DIRECTIONS:
Read each story. Then, read each question or statement and mark the space for the answer you think is right. Write your answer for number five on a separate sheet of paper.

Store keepers provide many things that people need. They bring different "goods" to one place where we can shop. Without store keepers, we would have to go many places to buy what we need.

1. This story is about people who own
   - goods
   - stores
   - needs

2. Store keepers bring many goods to one
   - place
   - house
   - truck

3. Store keepers bring together many things we
   - have
   - need
   - hate

4. As used in the story, the word "goods" means
   - ○ things to buy
   - ○ food
   - ○ stores

5. What are some of your favorite places to shop?

Neighbors are the people who live near you. You see these people almost every day. Neighbors help each other in many ways. They talk to each other and watch over the neighborhood.

1. People who live near you are
   - neighbors
   - friends
   - strangers

2. You probably see your neighbor at least once a
   - year
   - month
   - day

3. A neighbor who helps you is like a
   - teacher
   - friend
   - doctor

4. A good neighbor might do this when you are away
   - ○ have a big party
   - ○ do nothing
   - ○ watch your house

5. What have you done to help your neighbor?

Name _____   Skill: Expository Passages

DIRECTIONS:
Read each story. Then, read each question or statement and mark the space for the answer you think is right. Write your answer for number five on a separate sheet of paper.

When we are hungry but do not want to cook, we can go to a restaurant. We can sit down and wait while the food is cooked and brought to the table. We do not all have to eat the same thing.

1. We can go to a restaurant if we don't want to

   sit down   **cook**   **eat**
   ○   ○   ○

2. In some restaurants, you sit and wait at a

   table   **stove**   **hungry**
   ○   ○   ○

3. A restaurant is a place where we can buy

   meals   **groceries**   **water**
   ○   ○   ○

4. Something you could not order at a restaurant is
   ○ **cheese**
   ○ **books**
   ○ **meat**

5. Where is your favorite place to eat? Why?

Every community has a school. Teachers help us learn many new things. Together we read, write and do math every day. We need to learn these things to get a good job.

1. Children go to school to

   hide   **write**   **learn**
   ○   ○   ○

2. Who helps us at school?

   uncles   **teachers**   **sisters**
   ○   ○   ○

3. What does learning help us get when we are older?

   jobs   **birds**   **new things**
   ○   ○   ○

4. Which is something we might learn at school?
   ○ **how to cut logs**
   ○ **how to count by tens**
   ○ **how to sleep**

5. What subject do you like best? Why?

Name _____   Skill: Expository Passages

DIRECTIONS:
Read each story. Then, read each question or statement and mark the space for the answer you think is right. Write your answer for number five on a separate sheet of paper.

Want to read a book? Go to the library! Libraries have many books and tapes for you to borrow. You must bring the items back in a week or two so other people can use them, too.

1. What can you borrow from a library?
   - shoes
   - books
   - furniture

2. You can keep the books or tapes for one or two
   - weeks
   - months
   - years

3. Each book you borrow from the library costs
   - 50 cents
   - a dollar
   - nothing

4. The library is a good place to
   - ○ see a play
   - ○ study and find facts
   - ○ watch a parade

5. What is your favorite book? Why is it so good?

A hospital is a place we go if we are very sick or hurt. Doctors and nurses work there. They watch over you day and night. They give you medicine that helps to make you healthy again.

1. Who does not work in a hospital?
   - nurse
   - waitress
   - doctor

2. What do nurses bring to make you well?
   - food
   - candy
   - medicine

3. In a hospital you are always
   - alone
   - watched
   - hot

4. You should go to a hospital when you have
   - ○ a headache
   - ○ a cold
   - ○ a bad cut

5. Would you like to work in a hospital? Why or why not?

Name _____

Skill: Expository Passages

DIRECTIONS:
Read each story. Then, read each question or statement and mark the space for the answer you think is right. Write your answer for number five on a separate sheet of paper.

Your body has many parts. The outside is covered with skin that lets you feel things. You have arms and legs to help you move. You have eyes for seeing and ears for hearing.

1. With which part of the body do we see?

    ears   **eyes**   **arms**
    ○   ○   ○

2. What covers the outside of the body?

    legs   **arms**   **skin**
    ○   ○   ○

3. When you are tickled you

    feel it   **hear it**   **smell it**
    ○   ○   ○

4. Our arms and legs
    ○ **have a shell covering**
    ○ **help us to go**
    ○ **help us to hear things**

5. Which part of the body do you think is most important?

The heart is an organ inside your chest. It is about as big as your fist. The heart pumps blood to every part of your body. The blood carries things your body needs to work and grow.

1. The organ inside the chest is called the

    heart   **blood**   **body**
    ○   ○   ○

2. What does the heart pump?

    fist   **blood**   **chest**
    ○   ○   ○

3. What might the blood carry to our body parts?

    food   **anger**   **plants**
    ○   ○   ○

4. Your heart does not ever
    ○ **beat fast**
    ○ **help your body**
    ○ **take a rest**

5. What can you do to keep your heart healthy?

Name _____

Skill: Expository Passages

DIRECTIONS:
Read each story. Then, read each question or statement and mark the space for the answer you think is right. Write your answer for number five on a separate sheet of paper.

Do you take care of your body? Good food, lots of water, exercise, and rest can help your body stay strong and healthy. You must take care of your body so it can take care of you!

1. This story is about taking care of your
   - **body** ○
   - **food** ○
   - **hair** ○

2. One thing your body needs is
   - **heat** ○
   - **rest** ○
   - **candy** ○

3. Taking good care of your body is
   - **needless** ○
   - **smart** ○
   - **silly** ○

4. When you don't take care of your body, you might
   - ○ **get sick**
   - ○ **grow taller**
   - ○ **win a race**

5. What do you do to take care of your body?

Muscles need to be used if you want them to stay strong. Exercise is one way to use your muscles. Running, biking, skating, playing, and walking are all good ways to exercise your muscles.

1. What do your muscles need?
   - **water** ○
   - **sun** ○
   - **exercise** ○

2. Exercise will keep your muscles
   - **soft** ○
   - **strong** ○
   - **easy** ○

3. If your do not use your muscles, they will become
   - **weak** ○
   - **strong** ○
   - **bigger** ○

4. Running, skating, and walking are good ways to
   - ○ **rest**
   - ○ **take a bath**
   - ○ **exercise**

5. What is your favorite way to exercise? Why?

© Carson-Dellosa CD-3734

Name _____   Skill: Expository Passages

DIRECTIONS:
Read each story. Then, read each question or statement and mark the space for the answer you think is right. Write your answer for number five on a separate sheet of paper.

Does washing your hands help your body? Yes! Every day your hands pick up germs, tiny living things you can't see. Germs can make you sick. Washing your hands gets rid of most germs.

1. Tiny living things that you can't see are

   germs   **worms**   **hands**
   ○   ○   ○

2. We get germs on our hands every

   day   **week**   **month**
   ○   ○   ○

3. Washing your hands helps keep you

   sick   **healthy**   **sleepy**
   ○   ○   ○

4. What is the main idea of this story?
   ○ **germs are bad**
   ○ **keep your hands clean**
   ○ **take a bath**

5. How often should you wash your hands each day?

The clothes you wear can help keep your body healthy. You need to stay warm enough and dry. The clothes you wear can keep you warm or cool. They can also keep you dry in the rain!

1. Our bodies must stay dry and

   hot   **wet**   **warm**
   ○   ○   ○

2. Wearing clothes helps to keep our bodies

   healthy   **clean**   **cold**
   ○   ○   ○

3. What could you use to keep your body dry?

   sweater   **umbrella**   **swim suit**
   ○   ○   ○

4. What should you do if you get cold and wet?
   ○ **put on boots**
   ○ **drink something cool**
   ○ **put on dry clothes**

5. What is the best way to stay cool in the summer?

© Carson-Dellosa CD-3734

Name _____   Skill: Expository Passages

DIRECTIONS:
Read each story. Then, read each question or statement and mark the space for the answer you think is right. Write your answer for number five on a separate sheet of paper.

Teeth are important. Without them, we can not eat many of the foods our bodies need. Keep your teeth clean by brushing after every meal. Have a dentist look at them two times every year.

1. This story is about

   dentists **foods** **teeth**
   ○   ○   ○

2. How many times a year should you see the dentist?

   two   **three**   **five**
   ○   ○   ○

3. How many times a day should you brush?

   one   **two**   **three**
   ○   ○   ○

4. Without teeth we could not
   ○ **go to school**
   ○ **eat many types of food**
   ○ **walk**

5. What is the best thing to do for healthy teeth?

When you get sick, you might take medicine to make you well. It can be a shot, pills, or a drink. Some medicines keep us from catching an illness. Medicines can help us stay healthy.

1. We take medicine when we are

   sleepy   **old**   **sick**
   ○   ○   ○

2. You can take medicine as a drink, a shot, or a

   pill   **toy**   **meal**
   ○   ○   ○

3. Medicine helps us feel

   better   **hot**   **sick**
   ○   ○   ○

4. What is not a type of medicine?
   ○ **mumps**
   ○ **pills**
   ○ **a shot**

5. What kind of medicine do you like to take? Why?

Name _____   Skill: Letters

DIRECTIONS:
Read each letter. Then, read each question about the letter and mark the space for the answer you think is right. Write your answer for number 4 on a separate sheet of paper.

July 16, 1999
Dear Peg,
   My scout troop is having a picnic at the lake next Tuesday. We will play games, sing songs, and swim before we eat. We will have a big fire and cook our hotdogs over it. Would you like to come with me?
       Your friend,
       Sandy

August 6, 2000
Dear Lyle,
   I went on vacation with my family for three weeks. We camped in Yellowstone Park and saw many wild animals. A bear tried to get into our food box! Mom and I got into the car, but dad was in the tent. We were glad when the bear left!   Love,
       Peter

---

1. Who is this letter for?

   Peg   **Sandy**   **scouts**
   ○   ○   ○

2. What day is the picnic?

   July   **Tuesday**   **Friday**
   ○   ○   ○

3. What time of year is it?

   spring   **summer**   **fall**
   ○   ○   ○

4. What other things might scouts do together?

---

1. Who wrote this?

   Lyle   **Peter**   **Mom**
   ○   ○   ○

2. What is Yellowstone?

   bear   **park**   **vacation**
   ○   ○   ○

3. How did Peter feel when the bear came?

   happy   **scared**   **mad**
   ○   ○   ○

4. Would you go camping on your vacation? Why?

Name _____   Skill: Letters

DIRECTIONS:
Read each letter. Then, read each question about the letter and mark the space for the answer you think is right. Write your answer for number 4 on a separate sheet of paper.

September 8, 2000
Dear Mr. White,
   I did not mean to break your window. We were playing ball and I hit a home run over the fence. I did not know it would hit your house. I will pay to have the window fixed. I will be more careful next time.

     Sincerely,
     Frank

November 16, 1999
Dear Aunt Alice,
   Can you come to our house for Thanksgiving this year? We have a huge turkey and mom is making your favorite pie. We can watch the parades and eat all day! You can even bring your dog, Max, if you like.

     Your niece,
     Helen

---

1. What was Frank playing?

baseball   **tennis**   **soccer**
  ○   ○   ○

2. What was broken?

fence   **house**   **window**
  ○   ○   ○

3. What is Frank trying to tell Mr. White? He is

sorry   **glad**   **angry**
  ○   ○   ○

4. What do you think Mr. White might say to Frank?

---

1. Who wrote this letter?

Alice   **Max**   **Helen**
  ○   ○   ○

2. Thanksgiving is a

week   **holiday**   **parade**
  ○   ○   ○

3. Helen wrote this letter to Aunt Alice to say

miss you   **thank you**   **please come**
  ○   ○   ○

4. What do you think is Aunt Alice's favorite pie? Why?

© Carson-Dellosa CD-3734

Name _____   Skill: Letters

DIRECTIONS:
Read each letter. Then, read each question about the letter and mark the space for the answer you think is right. Write your answer for number 4 on a separate sheet of paper.

January 4, 2001
Dear Bob,
  I really like the present you gave me. I take very good care of him. I named him Fangs because he chews on everything. Fangs sleeps next to my bed at night. He purrs when I rub his ears. He is the best pet ever!
          Sincerely,
          Nick

March 27, 1999
Dear Mr. Broom,
  Joey does not have his work ready for school today. He had just started to do it last night when a monster knocked at our door. Joey let him in and the monster ate every bit of paper in the house! Joey will have it done tomorrow.
          Sincerely,
          Joey's Mom

1. Who gave the present?
   Nick **Fangs** **Bob**
   ○   ○   ○

2. What does Fangs like to do?
   eat **sleep** **chew**
   ○   ○   ○

3. What kind of pet is Fangs?
   dog **horse** **cat**
   ○   ○   ○

4. Is a pet a good gift to give? Why or why not?

1. When will Joey have his homework finished?
   next week **Friday** **tomorrow**
   ○   ○   ○

2. Who took the homework?
   Mr. Broom **Joey** **a monster**
   ○   ○   ○

3. Who is Mr. Broom?
   coach **teacher** **father**
   ○   ○   ○

4. Do you think Joey's mom really wrote this letter?

Name _____   Skill: Letters

DIRECTIONS:
Read each letter. Then, read each question about the letter and mark the space for the answer you think is right. Write your answer for number 4 on a separate sheet of paper.

> February 29, 2000
> Dear Elmer,
>   There is something very special about this day. Do you know what it is? This day only happens every four years. It is an extra day in February! This year is called Leap Year.
>
>   Your pal,
>   R.J.

> April 25, 2000
> Dear Julie,
>   I am having a party next Tuesday. Can you come? There will be colored balloons, cake, ice cream, and games. I will put eight candles on the cake, make a wish, then blow them out. Do you know what kind of party it is?
>   Please come,
>   Betty

---

1. Who wrote this letter?

   Elmer   **R.J.**   **February**
   ○   ○   ○

2. This special day comes once every

   year   **2 years**   **4 years**
   ○   ○   ○

3. How many days are usually in February?

   7   **28**   **29**
   ○   ○   ○

4. Which day of the year is your favorite? Why?

---

1. Betty is asking Julie to come to

   school   **a boat**   **a party**
   ○   ○   ○

2. When does Betty want her to come?

   today   **Tuesday**   **Saturday**
   ○   ○   ○

3. What kind of party is it?

   dance   **birthday**   **surprise**
   ○   ○   ○

4. What is the most fun thing to do at a party?

© Carson-Dellosa CD-3734

Answer Key

Name ____________________ Skill: Reading Words

DIRECTIONS:
Look at the picture in each box. Mark the word on each line that belongs with the picture.

1.	cookie ○	pizza ○	ice cream ●
2.	could ○	cold ●	warm ○
3.	cone ●	dish ○	cane ○

7.	bike ○	skates ●	sky ○
8.	wheels ●	well ○	wall ○
9.	rain ○	rip ○	roll ●

4.	shoe ●	sock ○	shot ○
5.	lane ○	lose ○	lace ●
6.	tie ●	ten ○	ton ○

SOAP

10.	sat ○	soup ○	soap ●
11.	bath ●	bite ○	boat ○
12.	clam ○	camp ○	clean ●

Name ____________________ Skill: Reading Words

DIRECTIONS:
Look at the picture in each box. Mark the word on each line that belongs with the picture.

1.	park ○	present ●	press ○
2.	bone ○	bow ●	back ○
3.	ribbon ●	robin ○	ran ○

7.	watch ●	witch ○	with ○
8.	had ○	happy ○	hands ●
9.	Tim ○	tore ○	time ●

4.	brush ●	bush ○	brave ○
5.	pan ○	past ○	paste ●
6.	teeth ●	told ○	tack ○

10.	trick ○	truck ○	tractor ●
11.	frame ○	farmer ●	fall ○
12.	tires ●	trim ○	tells ○

Name ____________________ Skill: Reading Words

DIRECTIONS:
Look at the picture in each box. Mark the word on each line that belongs with the picture.

1.	glad ○	globe ●	gone ○
2.	world ●	worm ○	wall ○
3.	Earth ●	Mars ○	sun ○

7.	boat ○	airplane ●	arm ○
8.	clip ○	could ○	clouds ●
9.	sack ○	skip ○	sky ●

4.	scarf ●	scare ○	sold ○
5.	cold ●	cost ○	class ○
6.	mittens ●	mind ○	kittens ○

10.	pal ○	puppy ●	pony ○
11.	bare ○	bone ●	blow ○
12.	wag ●	wig ○	win ○

Name ____________________ Skill: Reading Words

DIRECTIONS:
Look at each picture. Then, mark the word that best describes the picture on each line below it.

1.	drag ○	deer ○	dinosaur ●
2.	taste ○	tail ●	trail ○
3.	huge ●	hug ○	hop ○

7.	rink ○	rang ○	ring ●
8.	stone ●	stamp ○	slap ○
9.	city ○	round ●	come ○

4.	from ○	frog ●	fold ○
5.	pole ○	poor ○	pond ●
6.	flew ○	flower ●	feel ○

10.	basket ●	base ○	blade ○
11.	part ○	picnic ●	pick ○
12.	lamp ○	land ○	lunch ●

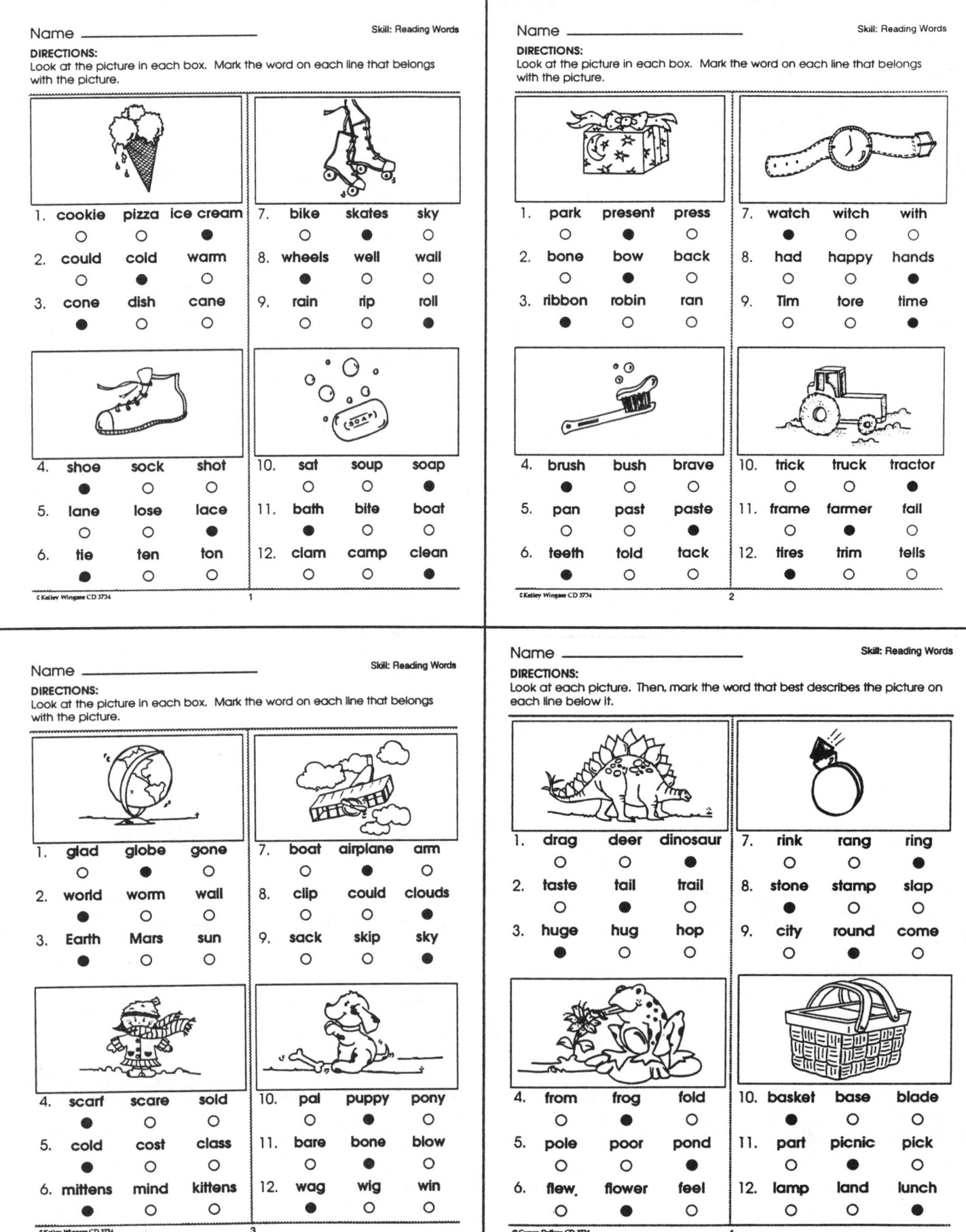

Answer Key

Page 5

Name _____ Skill: Reading Words

DIRECTIONS: Look at the picture in each box. Mark the word on each line that belongs with the picture.

Box 1 (sandcastle):
1. **castle** ●, cast ○, cake ○
2. flew ○, flow ○, **flag** ●
3. sit ○, stone ○, **sand** ●

Box 2 (cow):
7. crow ○, **cow** ●, call ○
8. **spots** ●, stops ○, spark ○
9. hold ○, **horns** ●, hall ○

Box 3 (crab):
4. candy ○, **crab** ●, cream ○
5. cape ○, **claw** ●, clue ○
6. **swim** ●, swing ○, sip ○

Box 4 (tree):
10. try ○, trim ○, **tree** ●
11. broke ○, **branch** ●, bank ○
12. **leaves** ●, lift ○, lend ○

Page 6

Name _____ Skill: Reading Words

DIRECTIONS: Look at the picture in each box. Mark the word on each line that belongs with the picture.

Box 1 (elephant):
1. **elephant** ●, egg ○, end ○
2. trick ○, tank ○, **trunk** ●
3. spin ○, **splash** ●, slap ○

Box 2 (calendar - January):
7. July ○, **January** ●, June ○
8. **month** ●, moth ○, mother ○
9. dent ○, **date** ●, damp ○

Box 3 (radio):
4. **radio** ●, road ○, ramp ○
5. mouth ○, **music** ●, maps ○
6. plan ○, past ○, **play** ●

Box 4 (beach):
10. bench ○, branch ○, **beach** ●
11. under ○, uncle ○, **umbrella** ●
12. **warm** ●, well ○, wing ○

Page 7

Name _____ Skill: Reading Words

DIRECTIONS: Look at the picture in each box. Mark the word on each line that belongs with the picture.

Box 1 (pizza):
1. pillow ○, pretty ○, **pizza** ●
2. safe ○, slip ○, **slice** ●
3. rope ○, robe ○, **round** ●

Box 2 (baby crawling):
7. bake ○, **baby** ●, bottom ○
8. **crawl** ●, crab ○, cut ○
9. sad ○, sleep ○, **smile** ●

Box 3 (swing set):
4. shell ○, swim ○, **swing** ●
5. **empty** ●, else ○, eight ○
6. **three** ●, four ○, five ○

Box 4 (picture/photo):
10. pick ○, **picture** ●, pants ○
11. **cap** ●, cup ○, cape ○
12. bend ○, bag ○, **boy** ●

Page 8

Name _____ Skill: Reading Words

DIRECTIONS: Look at the picture in each box. Mark the word on each line that belongs with the picture.

Box 1 (house):
1. hoop ○, hold ○, **house** ●
2. rope ○, **roof** ●, root ○
3. **smoke** ●, smile ○, smell ○

Box 2 (crown):
7. **crown** ●, crow ○, cart ○
8. pond ○, **point** ●, paint ○
9. quite ○, **squirrel** ●, queen ○

Box 3 (apple):
4. almost ○, any ○, **apple** ●
5. **fruit** ●, friend ○, file ○
6. **leaf** ●, left ○, laugh ○

Box 4 (snail):
10. sail ○, **snail** ●, snap ○
11. **shell** ●, shall ○, sell ○
12. **slow** ●, slid ○, slept ○

Answer Key

Name ____________________ Skill: Reading Words

DIRECTIONS:
Look at the picture in each box. Mark the word on each line that belongs with the picture.

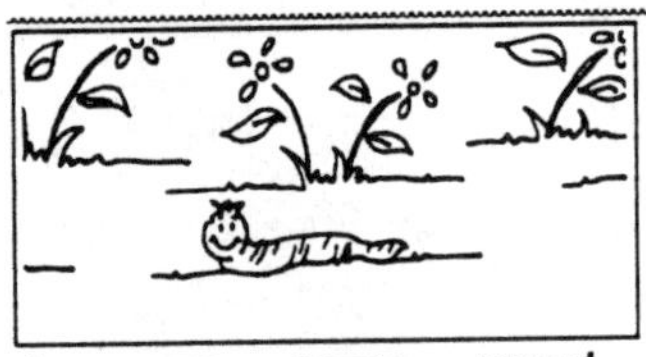

1. ● worm ○ warm ○ wand
2. ○ grew ○ gas ● grass
3. ● crawl ○ claw ○ clap

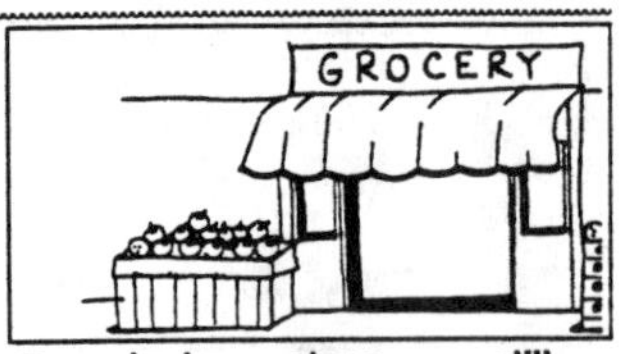
GROCERY

7. ○ start ● store ○ still
8. ● fruit ○ feet ○ fort
9. ○ sing ● sign ○ sand

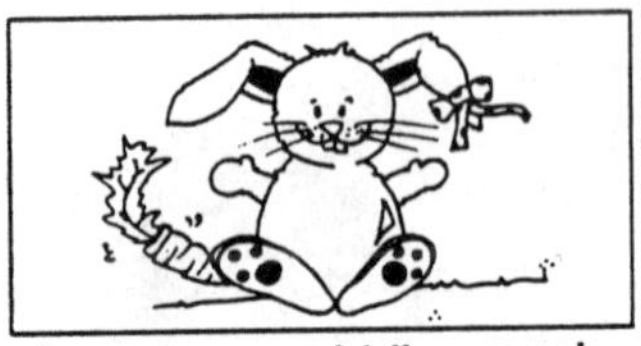

4. ○ rake ● rabbit ○ reach
5. ○ fold ● furry ○ find
6. ○ can ○ cart ● carrot

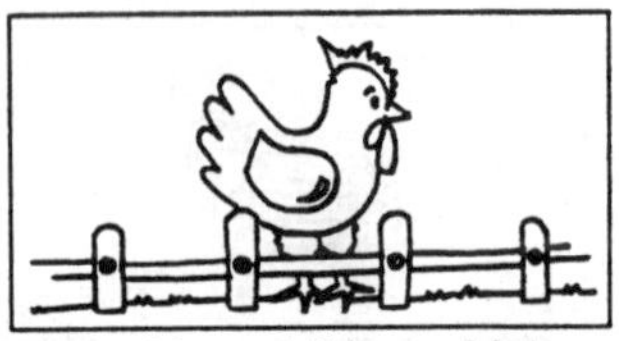

10. ○ chip ○ children ● chicken
11. ● fence ○ family ○ foot
12. ○ will ○ wand ● wing

Name ____________________ Skill: Reading Words

DIRECTIONS:
Look at the picture in each box. Mark the word on each line that belongs with the picture.

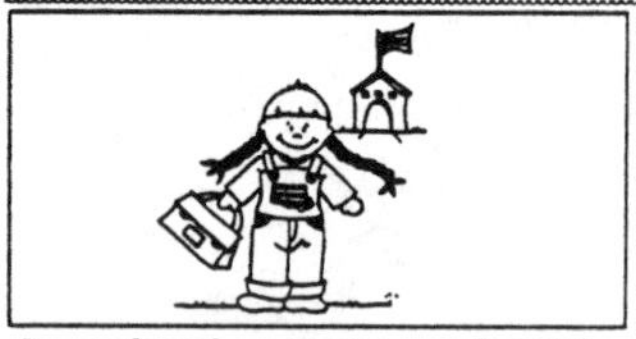

1. ● school ○ scare ○ should
2. ○ gift ○ grill ● girl
3. ○ circle ○ chew ● child

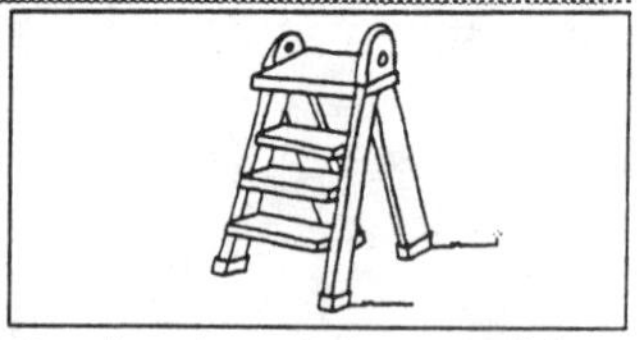

7. ○ lead ○ late ● ladder
8. ○ stops ○ shall ● steps
9. ● high ○ hang ○ held

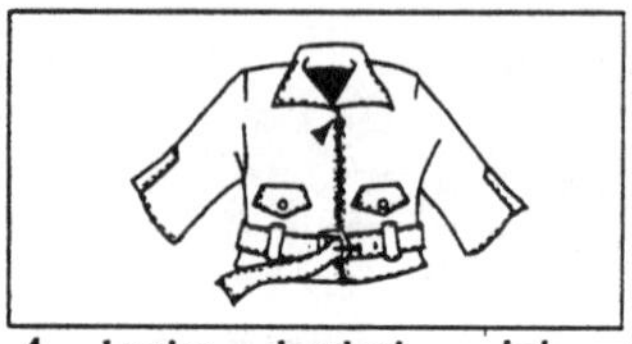

4. ○ jacks ● jacket ○ jet
5. ● belt ○ bold ○ band
6. ○ pack ○ pond ● pocket

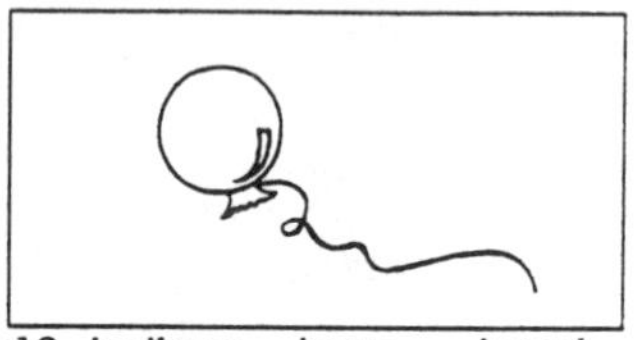

10. ● balloon ○ barn ○ bend
11. ○ sting ● string ○ stripe
12. ○ roller ○ rooster ● round

Name ____________________ Skill: Reading Words

DIRECTIONS:
Look at the picture in each box. Mark the word on each line that belongs with the picture.

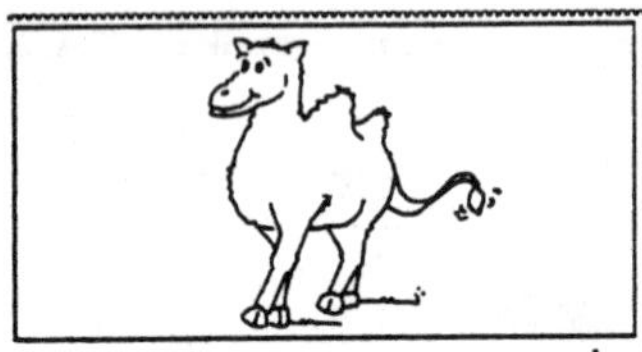

1. ○ cone ○ camp ● camel
2. ○ hand ○ hum ● humps
3. ○ wing ● walk ○ wake

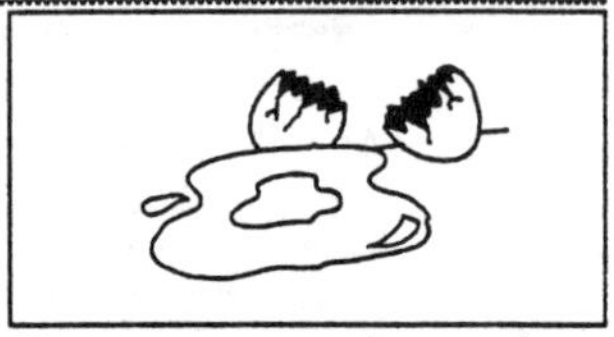

7. ● egg ○ each ○ enter
8. ○ blew ○ bread ● broken
9. ○ share ○ shall ● shell

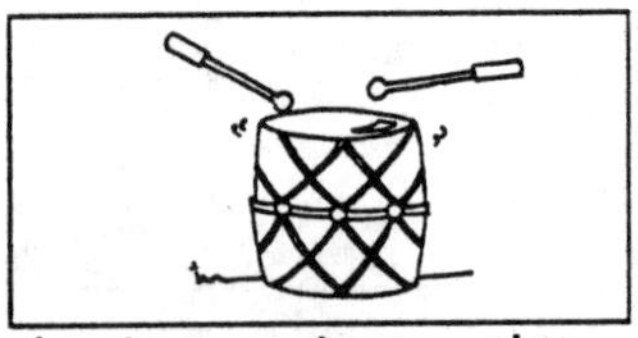

4. ● drum ○ drag ○ dug
5. ○ bull ○ bank ● bang
6. ● loud ○ cloud ○ lake

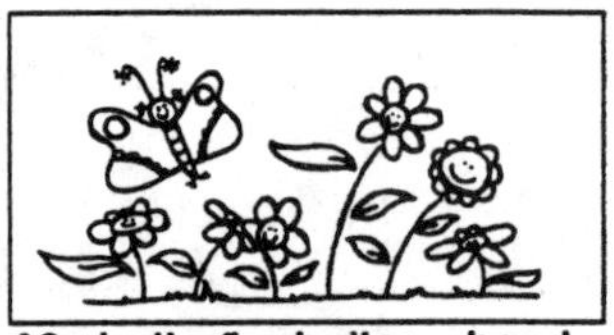

10. ● butterfly ○ butter ○ band
11. ○ flour ● flower ○ floor
12. ○ spell ● spring ○ spin

Name ____________________ Skill: Reading Words

DIRECTIONS:
Look at the picture in each box. Mark the word on each line that belongs with the picture.

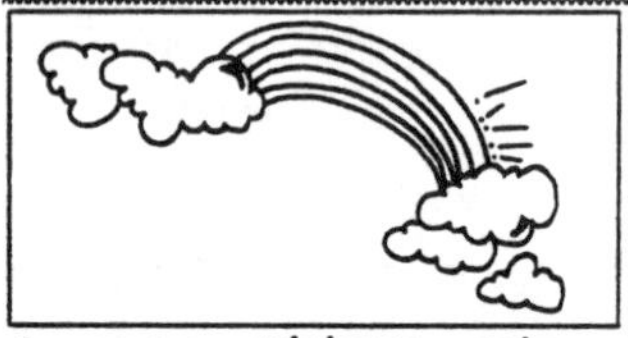

1. ○ ramp ● rainbow ○ rate
2. ● colors ○ coat ○ care
3. ○ clamp ● clouds ○ could

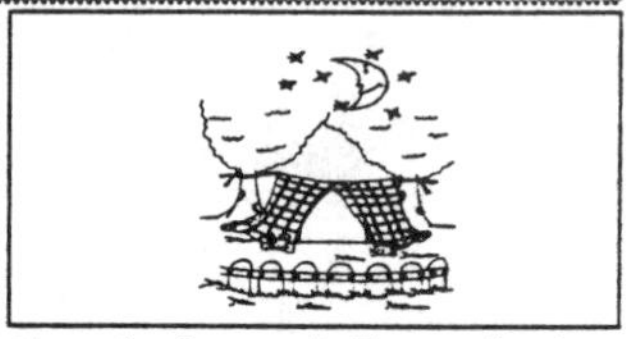

7. ○ test ○ tell ● tent
8. ○ cream ● camp ○ cast
9. ● yard ○ year ○ yell

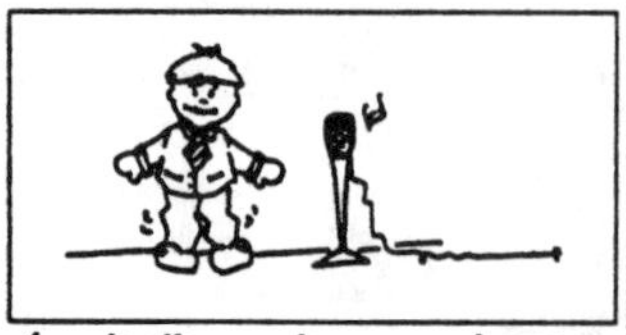

4. ○ both ● boy ○ bare
5. ● sing ○ sand ○ sun
6. ○ almost ○ add ● alone

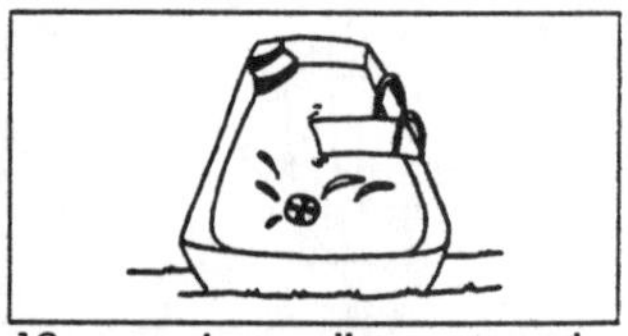

10. ● pool ○ pile ○ pond
11. ● float ○ flap ○ fire
12. ○ state ○ space ● splash

Answer Key

Page 13 — Skill: Reading Words

DIRECTIONS: Look at the picture in each box. Mark the word on each line that belongs with the picture.

1. dollar donkey **duck**
2. felt **feathers** family
3. **swim** sunny super

7. **lean** lend lamp
8. **flew** flap fall
9. **crash** crayon candle

4. gate grape **giant**
5. hard **huge** hung
6. **grab** gotten girl

10. **owl** own open
11. week **wing** wire
12. **bird** building bump

Page 14 — Skill: Word Study—Test 1

DIRECTIONS: One or more letters are underlined in each of the words below. Read each word, then mark the space under the answer choice that has the same sound as the underlined letter or letters.

1. act — **collect**, talk, bet
2. write — well, red, **bite**
3. boot — **fruit**, goat, hold
4. agree — **green**, gold, race
5. float — gone, flat, **note**
6. climb — plum, **limb**, limp
7. visit — **sight**, silver, swing

8. age — **giant**, go, give
9. bloom — bold, house, **room**
10. count — plan, **dent**, send
11. crow — cow, **go**, move
12. pile — pill, plant, **right**
13. charge — cage, **lunch**, heat
14. bump — mop, last, **jump**

Page 15 — Skill: Word Study Skills

DIRECTIONS: Each numbered word has underlined letters. Mark the space for the word that has the same sound as the letters that are underlined.

1. loud — **cow**, blow, pool
2. bench — class, bent, **change**
3. hang — **bring**, hand, catch
4. giant — together, **jump**, good
5. half — hall, gift, **calf**
6. afraid — feel, **friend**, raft
7. clay — **plate**, cry, pony

8. cricket — crown, **clock**, tooth
9. snap — slow, **snow**, show
10. shade — both, **brush**, snip
11. elephant — find, put, **please**
12. bar — stand, brand, **card**
13. fur — corn, fire, **nurse**
14. radio — bottle, ton, **open**

Page 16 — Skill: Word Study—Test 3

DIRECTIONS: One or more letters are underlined in each of the words below. Read each word, then mark the space under the answer choice that has the same sound as the underlined letter or letters.

1. bank — both, **pink**, been
2. cost — **stair**, cats, count
3. dragon — **get**, giant, drum
4. once — tone, **won**, no
5. band — **lend**, bent, slap
6. beyond — **yellow**, win, jog
7. breeze — extra, smile, **easy**

8. arm — chain, **farmer**, clam
9. free — **tree**, form, frame
10. paste — past, star, **mate**
11. moo — **you**, mouth, put
12. enough — give, **fall**, goat
13. ranch — ramp, **chip**, clip
14. doghouse — hose, **mouth**, poor

Answer Key

Page 17

Skill: Word Study Skills

DIRECTIONS: Each numbered word has underlined letters. Mark the space for the word that has the same sound as the letters that are underlined.

1. clo**th** — math ●
2. ch**ir**p — bird ●
3. c**a**ge — orange ●
4. **kn**ee — can ●
5. prob**l**em — blend ●
6. **dr**um — umbrella ●
7. **pr**ess — prune ●
8. **e**mpty — them ●
9. c**or**n — morning ●
10. blo**ck** — cricket ●
11. m**ar**k — pork ●
12. **qu**ack — crack ●
13. **pl**ain — play ●
14. a**sl**eep — slip ●

Page 18

Skill: Word Study Skills

1. a**g**ainst — past ●
2. c**a**ndle — lamp ●
3. pr**ou**d — loud ●
4. bo**ss** — grass ●
5. m**i**lk — silk ●
6. bod**y** — meet ●
7. colle**ct** — fact ●
8. de**s**k — skate ●
9. **ch**in — chip ●
10. b**a**sket — scare ●
11. ke**pt** — slept ●
12. p**ay** — made ●
13. arti**st** — slap ●
14. **th**in — both ●

Page 19

Skill: Word Study Skills

1. **sw**am — sweet ●
2. bri**ng** — string ●
3. broke**n** — neck ●
4. b**u**g — jump ●
5. j**o**ke — hole ●
6. sh**y** — cry ●
7. b**ea**ch — eat ●
8. **bl**ew — you ●
9. c**a**se — gain ●
10. **fl**ap — flower ●
11. b**or**n — storm ●
12. d**o**ne — stone ●
13. **b**et — tab ●
14. **ear**ly — eat ●

Page 20

Skill: Word Study Skills

1. **cl**ap — climb ●
2. t**oe** — no ●
3. **sm**art — mist ●
4. **tr**ail — brand ●
5. **c**ircus — same ●
6. **g**ate — tale ●
7. b**ro**ke — cold ●
8. d**ir**t — bird ●
9. ba**ng** — ring ●
10. **p**urple — nurse ●
11. **br**ace — about ●
12. **ch**icken — chap ●
13. t**u**na — fruit ●
14. **c**ap — pace ●

Answer Key

Name ____________________ Skill: Word Study Skills

DIRECTIONS:
Each numbered word has underlined letters. Mark the space for the word that has the same sound as the letters that are underlined.

1. dash	shop ●	dip ○	both ○
2. farm	phone ●	harm ○	pull ○
3. meat	mat ○	bet ○	beet ●
4. clue	purple ○	pump ○	rule ●
5. blow	top ○	more ○	poke ●
6. left	feel ○	felt ○	lift ●
7. point	pool ○	toy ●	spoon ○
8. camp	pan ○	limp ●	came ○
9. slide	asleep ●	sheep ○	lid ○
10. bend	bent ○	from ○	friend ●
11. curl	turkey ●	cramp ○	glad ○
12. bush	fist ○	shut ●	snip ○
13. space	skip ○	wasp ●	sap ○
14. any	cry ○	teeth ●	yellow ○

Name ____________________ Skill: Word Study Skills

DIRECTIONS:
Each numbered word has underlined letters. Mark the space for the word that has the same sound as the letters that are underlined.

1. different	damp ○	tent ●	tend ○
2. extra	zip ○	exit ●	tell ○
3. between	twin ●	spin ○	swing ○
4. drive	give ○	indoor ○	drip ●
5. copy	story ●	yarn ○	cape ○
6. catch	chat ○	want ○	watch ●
7. breath	path ●	turn ○	beat ○
8. grab	garden ○	grass ●	bag ○
9. bare	brag ○	car ○	care ●
10. bridge	bread ○	judge ●	great ○
11. caught	fall ○	laugh ○	light ●
12. bet	tan ○	nab ●	net ○
13. black	chick ○	ball ○	block ●
14. child	lid ○	gold ●	chick ○

Name ____________________ Skill: Spelling

DIRECTIONS:
Read each group of words. Mark the word that is **not** spelled correctly.

1. ○ plant ● truk ○ beautiful ○ draw
2. ○ drink ○ horse ● onle ○ soon
3. ○ sorry ○ what's ● undr ○ began
4. ○ begin ○ ever ○ paint ● sqirrel
5. ○ bet ○ burn ● clasroom ○ deep
6. ○ hop ○ off ○ song ● wel'l
7. ○ wet ● aneway ○ rabbit ○ two
8. ● eveen ○ hurt ○ outside ○ sound
9. ○ while ○ beside ○ bunny ● clappe
10. ○ flap ● goodnes ○ hung ○ lead
11. ○ anyone ○ put ○ turtle ● becuz
12. ○ been ○ drove ● hunrgy ○ our
13. ● wich ○ apart ○ rain ○ us
14. ○ decide ● eigt ○ five ○ golden
15. ● betwen ○ bush ○ clay ○ deer

Name ____________________ Skill: Spelling

DIRECTIONS:
Read each group of words. Mark the word that is **not** spelled correctly.

1. ○ road ○ very ○ being ● evryone
2. ○ part ○ star ● winde ○ arrow
3. ○ bike ○ eye ○ keep ● pickture
4. ○ plan ● stepe ○ without ○ asleep
5. ○ pot ○ stone ● wurd ○ awake
6. ● insied ○ pan ○ stand ○ white
7. ○ sad ○ walk ○ better ● partey
8. ○ stay ○ wish ● artest ○ sat
9. ○ bit ○ family ○ king ● pleese
10. ● seede ○ went ○ black ○ faster
11. ● rok ○ wait ○ best ○ isn't
12. ○ start ● wintter ○ same ○ was
13. ○ water ● brithday ○ face ○ kind
14. ○ stick ○ wood ○ aunt ● skool
15. ○ kitten ○ pound ● stoore ○ worker

Answer Key

Name _____   Skill: Spelling

DIRECTIONS:
Read each group of words. Mark the word that is **not** spelled correctly.

1. ● babby
   ○ show
   ○ were
   ○ boat

2. ○ bone
   ● felle
   ○ leg
   ○ push

3. ● reddy
   ○ table
   ○ zoo
   ○ bang

4. ○ small
   ○ won't
   ○ bus
   ● flor

5. ○ long
   ● roum
   ○ teacher
   ○ bare

6. ○ feed
   ○ leave
   ● prety
   ○ story

7. ● stuk
   ○ yellow
   ○ balloon
   ○ sleep

8. ○ slow
   ○ woman
   ○ brown
   ● furst

9. ○ line
   ○ right
   ● talle
   ○ bar

10. ● wud
    ○ care
    ○ food
    ○ love

11. ● yel
    ○ backyard
    ○ sing
    ○ when

12. ○ window
    ○ brother
    ○ fine
    ● ledder

13. ● ligth
    ○ real
    ○ tail
    ○ bank

14. ● sume
    ○ work
    ○ cake
    ○ flower

15. ○ rope
    ○ than
    ○ barn
    ● your'e

25

Name _____   Skill: Spelling

DIRECTIONS:
Read each group of words. Mark the word that is **not** spelled correctly.

1. ○ cave
   ○ gave
   ● lunnch
   ○ sandy

2. ○ sang
   ● abouve
   ○ baseball
   ○ street

3. ● thos
   ○ act
   ○ basket
   ○ need

4. ○ swim
   ● clos
   ○ gone
   ○ might

5. ● mixt
   ○ shoe
   ○ told
   ○ against

6. ● thier
   ○ able
   ○ base
   ○ still

7. ○ children
   ○ glad
   ○ these
   ● ackross

8. ● suprise
   ○ gold
   ○ clean
   ○ men

9. ○ seen
   ○ tire
   ● afrade
   ○ beach

10. ○ talk
    ○ again
    ● clouwn
    ○ grass

11. ○ youth
    ○ chair
    ○ give
    ● makeing

12. ● namme
    ○ class
    ○ mean
    ○ seat

13. ● sekret
    ○ tiger
    ○ add
    ○ bath

14. ○ next
    ○ take
    ○ cloud
    ● gramda

15. ○ mom
    ○ shop
    ● tonite
    ○ age

26

Name _____   Skill: Spelling

DIRECTIONS:
Read each group of words. Mark the word that is **not** spelled correctly.

1. ○ tell
   ○ ago
   ○ great
   ● monney

2. ○ morning
   ○ shout
   ○ toy
   ● ahede

3. ○ air
   ● bedrume
   ○ them
   ○ always

4. ○ another
   ○ cook
   ○ hand
   ● mouve

5. ○ think
   ○ any
   ● countree
   ○ head

6. ● shuld
   ○ town
   ○ agree
   ○ became

7. ● becum
   ○ that's
   ○ along
   ○ color

8. ● comming
   ○ guess
   ○ move
   ○ sign

9. ○ sister
   ○ tried
   ○ alike
   ● befor

10. ● miself
    ○ six
    ○ alley
    ○ behind

11. ○ thank
    ○ alone
    ○ cold
    ● greew

12. ○ ground
    ● moste
    ○ side
    ○ track

13. ○ train
    ● airplan
    ○ bedtime
    ○ then

14. ● could'nt
    ○ he's
    ○ six
    ○ trip

15. ○ thought
    ○ cry
    ○ hear
    ● nammed

27

Name _____   Skill: Spelling

DIRECTIONS:
Read each group of words. Mark the word that is **not** spelled correctly.

1. ○ smell
   ○ try
   ● allmost
   ○ believe

2. ○ bell
   ● tooday
   ○ aren't
   ○ dark

3. ○ nice
   ○ snow
   ○ use
   ● anser

4. ○ bench
   ○ pick
   ○ tree
   ● bakke

5. ● plase
   ○ trick
   ○ bark
   ○ done

6. ○ three
   ● applle
   ○ dance
   ○ heard

7. ○ helper
   ○ never
   ● aslo
   ○ belong

8. ○ top
   ○ ate
   ● doktor
   ○ noise

9. ● doe'snt
   ○ hold
   ○ hole
   ○ note

10. ● elefant
    ○ flash
    ○ gotten
    ○ hunt

11. ● neer
    ○ smile
    ○ turn
    ○ already

12. ○ took
    ● arund
    ○ dinner
    ○ herself

13. ○ nose
    ○ someday
    ● was'nt
    ○ anybody

14. ● somone
    ○ watch
    ○ anymore
    ○ bend

15. ● leaff
    ○ meat
    ○ beyond
    ○ clear

28

Answer Key

Page 29 — Skill: Spelling

DIRECTIONS: Read each group of words. Mark the word that is **not** spelled correctly.

1. ● deskt
   ○ flat
   ○ grab
   ○ lean

2. ● buterfly
   ○ die
   ○ flip
   ○ click

3. ○ ice
   ● lether
   ○ blew
   ○ buy

4. ● blok
   ○ cage
   ○ cloth
   ○ dine

5. ● durt
   ○ enter
   ○ fold
   ○ grown

6. ○ butter
   ○ clever
   ○ else
   ● fleew

7. ○ grandfather
   ○ learn
   ● blankat
   ○ button

8. ○ clock
   ○ dig
   ○ enemy
   ● flud

9. ● enuff
   ○ flour
   ○ growl
   ○ important

10. ● indeed
    ○ lemon
    ○ midle
    ○ blow

11. ● graid
    ○ hurry
    ○ leap
    ○ melt

12. ● clim
    ○ empty
    ○ different
    ○ float

13. ○ gray
    ○ idea
    ● ledd
    ○ met

14. ○ left
    ○ mice
    ● bluum
    ○ camp

15. ○ candle
    ● clu
    ○ dish
    ○ evening

Page 30 — Skill: Spelling

DIRECTIONS: Read each group of words. Mark the word that is **not** spelled correctly.

1. ● folow
   ○ indoor
   ○ lesson
   ○ mile

2. ● boddie
   ○ cannot
   ○ coin
   ○ doghouse

3. ● forerest
   ○ half
   ○ invite
   ○ mind

4. ○ boss
   ○ card
   ○ cool
   ● doun

5. ○ forgot
   ○ hang
   ● lissen
   ○ mirror

6. ○ board
   ○ candy
   ○ dive
   ● everbody

7. ○ foot
   ○ hair
   ○ interest
   ● licke

8. ○ born
   ● captin
   ○ cookie
   ○ dollar

9. ○ forget
   ● hamer
   ○ itself
   ○ lift

10. ● botle
    ○ carrot
    ○ corn
    ○ doorbell

11. ○ fool
    ○ instead
    ● libary
    ○ milk

12. ○ boot
    ○ cap
    ○ collect
    ● eskact

13. ○ forever
    ● iland
    ○ life
    ○ mine

14. ○ both
    ● carefull
    ○ copy
    ○ donkey

15. ○ happen
    ● jarr
    ○ lock
    ○ moan

Page 31 — Skill: Spelling

DIRECTIONS: Read each group of words. Mark the word that is **not** spelled correctly.

1. ● bottom
   ○ carry
   ○ corner
   ○ doorway

2. ● staje
   ○ pail
   ○ young
   ○ straw

3. ○ press
   ○ sandwich
   ○ sight
   ● sentense

4. ○ ugly
   ● spreed
   ○ travel
   ○ second

5. ● vegtable
   ○ sense
   ○ sail
   ○ office

6. ● nonne
   ○ pen
   ○ root
   ○ she'll

7. ○ sale
   ● sholder
   ○ radio
   ○ plate

8. ○ third
   ○ slid
   ● policce
   ○ return

9. ○ print
   ● prinse
   ○ sack
   ○ purple

10. ○ strange
    ● ritch
    ○ shade
    ○ rice

11. ○ vine
    ● wunder
    ○ penny
    ○ north

12. ● zoome
    ○ tape
    ○ quite
    ○ worry

13. ○ whole
    ● sumer
    ○ safe
    ○ popcorn

14. ○ pony
    ○ slide
    ○ smart
    ● wize

15. ○ unhappy
    ○ wave
    ● quession
    ○ shut

Page 32 — Skill: Synonyms

DIRECTIONS: Read the sentences and answer choices below. Mark the word or phrase that means almost the same thing as the word or phrase that is underlined in the sentence.

1. The <u>Earth</u> is round.
   ○ dirt
   ● planet
   ○ eat

2. Those <u>women</u> are having a meeting.
   ○ men
   ○ children
   ● ladies

3. I can't believe you ate <u>the whole</u> pie.
   ● all of
   ○ none of
   ○ some of

4. Sue will <u>welcome</u> the guests at the door.
   ● greet
   ○ say goodbye to
   ○ close

5. We had a <u>wonderful</u> time at the party.
   ● great
   ○ awful
   ○ terrible

6. My father is a <u>wise</u> man.
   ○ old
   ● smart
   ○ small

7. Gus can work <u>whenever</u> you need him.
   ○ today
   ○ never
   ● any time

8. We will <u>go to see</u> my grandma at Thanksgiving.
   ○ wonder
   ○ worry
   ● visit

Answer Key

Page 33 — Skill: Synonyms

DIRECTIONS: Read the sentences and answer choices below. Mark the word or phrase that means almost the same thing as the word or phrase that is underlined in the sentence.

1. Can you <u>reach</u> the top shelf?
   - ○ travel
   - ○ ranch
   - ● touch

2. Set your books <u>upon</u> the table.
   - ○ under
   - ○ over
   - ● on top of

3. I <u>see</u> what you mean!
   - ● understand
   - ○ don't get
   - ○ join

4. Please do not <u>tug</u> on my jacket.
   - ○ touch
   - ● pull
   - ○ poke

5. I live in a small <u>village</u> near the ocean.
   - ○ house
   - ● town
   - ○ country

6. Joe was <u>sad</u> when his puppy ran away.
   - ● unhappy
   - ○ glad
   - ○ silly

7. Our muddy shoes made the floor look <u>ugly</u>.
   - ○ shiny
   - ○ brown
   - ● not pretty

8. The policeman will <u>catch</u> the thief.
   - ● trap
   - ○ see
   - ○ call to

Page 34 — Skill: Synonyms

DIRECTIONS: Read the sentences and answer choices below. Mark the word or phrase that means almost the same thing as the word or phrase that is underlined in the sentence.

1. The boys hiked down the mountain <u>trail</u>.
   - ○ stones
   - ○ side
   - ● path

2. I will call you <u>tomorrow</u>.
   - ○ the day before today
   - ● the day after today
   - ○ next week

3. It is such a <u>sunny</u> day today!
   - ● bright
   - ○ cloudy
   - ○ cold

4. I had a really <u>bad</u> day!
   - ○ different
   - ○ good
   - ● terrible

5. I like to <u>touch</u> that soft blanket.
   - ○ sleep under
   - ● feel
   - ○ fold

6. The spider we caught is very <u>tiny</u>.
   - ○ ugly
   - ○ hairy
   - ● small

7. Be careful so you won't <u>tear</u> your jacket.
   - ● rip
   - ○ patch
   - ○ miss

8. Will you <u>toss</u> the baseball to me?
   - ○ hit
   - ● throw
   - ○ through

Page 35 — Skill: Synonyms—Test 4

DIRECTIONS: Read each of the sentences below. Then, mark the word or phrase that means almost the same thing as the word or phrase that is underlined.

1. That snake is about to <u>strike</u> the mouse.
   - ● bite
   - ○ play with
   - ○ avoid

2. My cat can <u>spring</u> to the table easily.
   - ○ fall
   - ○ flip
   - ● jump

3. Draw a <u>box</u> around the correct answer.
   - ○ round
   - ● square
   - ○ circle

4. Please <u>shut</u> the door when you leave.
   - ○ open
   - ○ knock on
   - ● close

5. Please <u>pile</u> your books neatly on the desk.
   - ● stack
   - ○ pick up
   - ○ have

6. Mother <u>spoke</u> to us about doing our homework soon.
   - ● talked
   - ○ yelled
   - ○ whispered

7. I have a <u>bright</u> new penny!
   - ○ cent
   - ○ dull
   - ● shiny

8. I ate too much and now feel a little <u>ill</u>.
   - ● sick
   - ○ tired
   - ○ unhappy

Page 36 — Skill: Synonyms

DIRECTIONS: Read the sentences and answer choices below. Mark the word or phrase that means almost the same thing as the word or phrase that is underlined in the sentence.

1. Sally will pull the sheets until they are <u>flat</u> on the bed.
   - ○ wrinkled
   - ● smooth
   - ○ over

2. Put some <u>dirt</u> in the pot so we can plant the flower.
   - ● soil
   - ○ seeds
   - ○ water

3. Please <u>rush</u> this letter to the postman.
   - ● hurry
   - ○ mail
   - ○ ready

4. Will you <u>save</u> my place in line, please?
   - ● keep
   - ○ give away
   - ○ stop

5. The dog stopped to <u>sniff</u> the trash can.
   - ○ bark at
   - ○ pull over
   - ● smell

6. The skin on a toad feels <u>rough</u>.
   - ○ smooth
   - ● bumpy
   - ○ hard

7. I will carry the doughnuts in a <u>sack</u>.
   - ○ paper
   - ○ pail
   - ● bag

8. I did not mean to <u>frighten</u> you.
   - ○ fix
   - ● scare
   - ○ stare at

Answer Key

Name _____ Skill: Synonyms

DIRECTIONS:
Read the sentences and answer choices below. Mark the word or phrase that means almost the same thing as the word or phrase that is underlined in the sentence.

1. I will seek the answer to that question.
   - ○ forget
   - ○ give
   - ● look for

2. I can sense that you are angry with me.
   - ● feel
   - ○ sad
   - ○ look

3. I am quick with my math facts!
   - ● fast
   - ○ smart
   - ○ slow

4. I must return my books to the library.
   - ○ borrow
   - ● take back
   - ○ buy

5. Do not yell at your little sister!
   - ○ slap
   - ● scream
   - ○ smile

6. I will question the man who saw what happened.
   - ○ listen to
   - ● ask
   - ○ know

7. I need to repair my broken radio.
   - ○ throw away
   - ○ sell
   - ● fix

8. Nan will phone us later today.
   - ○ shout
   - ● call
   - ○ see

Name _____ Skill: Synonyms

DIRECTIONS:
Read the sentences and answer choices below. Mark the word or phrase that means almost the same thing as the word or phrase that is underlined in the sentence.

1. Do you have a present for Bob?
   - ● gift
   - ○ box
   - ○ wrap

2. My frog can jump about three feet!
   - ● leap
   - ○ slide
   - ○ swim

3. The store is nearby.
   - ○ away
   - ○ far
   - ● close

4. Did you pass the red fence on the way here?
   - ● go by
   - ○ hand over
   - ○ climb

5. Did you notice that I got my hair cut?
   - ● see
   - ○ like
   - ○ feel

6. At the beginning of the race, Hal was ahead.
   - ○ behind
   - ● in the lead
   - ○ second

7. Put the flowers in the center of the table.
   - ○ side
   - ● middle
   - ○ back

8. Do not peek until I tell you!
   - ○ talk
   - ○ wake
   - ● look

Name _____ Skill: Synonyms

DIRECTIONS:
Read the sentences and answer choices below. Mark the word or phrase that means almost the same thing as the word or phrase that is underlined in the sentence.

1. I will raise the window to let in fresh air.
   - ● lift
   - ○ high
   - ○ under

2. Jim wants the blue ball instead of the red one.
   - ○ because
   - ○ as well as
   - ● in place of

3. The book was hidden behind the chair.
   - ○ placed
   - ● out of sight
   - ○ going

4. Bill made a giant pile of leaves when he raked.
   - ● large
   - ○ loose
   - ○ small

5. I didn't listen to the music that was playing.
   - ○ talk
   - ● hear
   - ○ earn

6. Will you invite Robert to your party?
   - ○ joke
   - ○ bring
   - ● ask

7. The bears lived deep in the dark forest.
   - ● woods
   - ○ mountains
   - ○ tree

8. The lights went out just as I entered the room.
   - ○ ran to
   - ○ went past
   - ● went into

Name _____ Skill: Synonyms

DIRECTIONS:
Read the sentences and answer choices below. Mark the word or phrase that means almost the same thing as the word or phrase that is underlined in the sentence.

1. I bent the tree branch too far and it snapped.
   - ○ twisted
   - ● broke
   - ○ grew

2. I have a pair of red shoes.
   - ● two
   - ○ four
   - ○ one

3. The class was very loud while the teacher was gone.
   - ○ quiet
   - ○ wonderful
   - ● noisy

4. Sue was certain that the coat was hers.
   - ○ happy
   - ● sure
   - ○ right

5. I have one cent to put in my bank.
   - ○ dollar
   - ● penny
   - ○ dime

6. This dress is perfect for the party.
   - ○ too small
   - ○ colorful
   - ● just right

7. I must hurry or I will be late!
   - ● go fast
   - ○ wait
   - ○ hold

8. Put the cover on the pan so you don't get burned.
   - ● lid
   - ○ lip
   - ○ pot

Answer Key

Page 41
Skill: Antonyms

DIRECTIONS: Read the sentences and answer choices below. Mark the word that means the opposite of the word that is underlined in the sentence.

1. <u>Anyone</u> can come to the dance.
   - ● no one
   - ○ everyone
   - ○ some

2. I was <u>asleep</u> at ten o'clock last night.
   - ○ rest
   - ● awake
   - ○ eating

3. Do you have a swing in your <u>backyard</u>?
   - ● front yard
   - ○ house
   - ○ yard

4. Put the old boxes in the <u>attic</u>.
   - ○ garage
   - ○ bedroom
   - ● basement

5. Keep those two dogs <u>apart</u> or they will fight.
   - ○ over
   - ○ away
   - ● together

6. My <u>aunt</u> gave me a bike for my birthday.
   - ○ lady
   - ○ grandmother
   - ● uncle

7. The family in the story was very <u>poor</u>.
   - ○ nice
   - ● rich
   - ○ mean

8. I will read a book <u>after</u> I take a bath.
   - ○ while
   - ● before
   - ○ soon

Page 42
Skill: Antonyms

1. Janice was <u>behind</u> Ted in the lunch line.
   - ○ beside
   - ○ next to
   - ● ahead of

2. Do you want to <u>add</u> anything to the drawing?
   - ○ give
   - ● take away
   - ○ say

3. Will you vote <u>for</u> John as class president?
   - ○ with
   - ● against
   - ○ open

4. I was so <u>happy</u> when I heard the news.
   - ○ pleased
   - ● sad
   - ○ silly

5. Put your hat on the shelf <u>above</u> the coats.
   - ● below
   - ○ over
   - ○ behind

6. There are times when I am very <u>brave</u>.
   - ● afraid
   - ○ bold
   - ○ mean

7. We are <u>alike</u> in many ways!
   - ● different
   - ○ the same
   - ○ friends

8. Wrap the present in <u>plain</u> paper.
   - ○ white
   - ○ flat
   - ● fancy

Page 43
Skill: Antonyms

1. <u>Both</u> of us were glad to get home.
   - ● neither
   - ○ two
   - ○ all

2. Judy <u>bought</u> six toys at the yard sale.
   - ● sold
   - ○ gave
   - ○ had

3. Did you <u>break</u> the glass in the window?
   - ○ crack
   - ● fix
   - ○ glue

4. Bring water <u>to</u> the picnic.
   - ● from
   - ○ on
   - ○ when

5. Is this the <u>bottom</u> of the box?
   - ○ end
   - ○ side
   - ● top

6. I was very <u>brave</u> when the cat jumped out at me.
   - ○ nice
   - ○ happy
   - ● scared

7. I found a <u>bright</u> penny in the grass.
   - ● dull
   - ○ new
   - ○ shiny

8. This is a <u>short</u> story.
   - ○ good
   - ● long
   - ○ small

Page 44
Skill: Antonyms

1. I <u>gave</u> a present.
   - ○ have
   - ○ see
   - ● took

2. Will your dad <u>buy</u> that car?
   - ○ paint
   - ○ drive
   - ● sell

3. Tim was <u>careful</u> with the glass plate.
   - ○ safe
   - ● careless
   - ○ hungry

4. I was <u>certain</u> I left the book on the table!
   - ○ easy
   - ● not sure
   - ○ told

5. Jill has a <u>few</u> holes in her socks.
   - ○ two
   - ○ some
   - ● many

6. I <u>cannot</u> go to the movie with you.
   - ○ doesn't
   - ● will
   - ○ won't

7. Did you <u>catch</u> the ball?
   - ● drop
   - ○ hold
   - ○ hit

8. The crowd began to <u>cheer</u> for the team.
   - ○ laugh
   - ○ yell for
   - ● boo

Answer Key

Page 45 — Skill: Antonyms

DIRECTIONS: Read the sentences and answer choices below. Mark the word that means the opposite of the word that is underlined in the sentence.

1. The fox was very <u>clever</u> in this story!
   - ● dumb
   - ○ smart
   - ○ fluffy

2. It is a little <u>warm</u> outside today.
   - ○ rainy
   - ○ hot
   - ● cool

3. Julie was <u>angry</u> because she lost her boot.
   - ● happy
   - ○ sad
   - ○ tired

4. We will set up the tent in the <u>daytime</u>.
   - ○ shade
   - ○ noon
   - ● night time

5. Will you <u>collect</u> the lunch money now?
   - ○ pick up
   - ● give out
   - ○ pack

6. I had to <u>crawl</u> across the room.
   - ● walk
   - ○ look
   - ○ creep

7. My <u>daughter</u> goes to your school.
   - ○ child
   - ● son
   - ○ sister

8. Please <u>shut</u> the door as you leave the room.
   - ○ close
   - ● open
   - ○ slam

Page 46 — Skill: Antonyms

DIRECTIONS: Read the sentences and answer choices below. Mark the word that means the opposite of the word that is underlined in the sentence.

1. Feed the plant a lot if you want it to <u>live</u>.
   - ● die
   - ○ grow
   - ○ turn green

2. Will you <u>fill</u> a big hole for me?
   - ○ dirt
   - ● dig
   - ○ jump in

3. After the big storm, I was <u>dry</u>!
   - ○ hot
   - ○ cold
   - ● wet

4. Is that glass <u>empty</u>?
   - ○ broken
   - ● full
   - ○ ugly

5. Would you like a seat that is <u>different</u>?
   - ○ not the same
   - ○ higher
   - ● the same

6. Do not <u>drop</u> the baby!
   - ○ play with
   - ● lift
   - ○ sit on

7. Please don't come to my house too <u>early</u>.
   - ● late
   - ○ soon
   - ○ quick

8. That boy is my <u>friend</u>.
   - ○ cousin
   - ○ pal
   - ● enemy

Page 47 — Skill: Antonyms

DIRECTIONS: Read the sentences and answer choices below. Mark the word that means the opposite of the word that is underlined in the sentence.

1. Can you get any <u>closer</u>?
   - ○ nearer
   - ● farther
   - ○ front

2. This is the <u>first</u> time I will write this story.
   - ● final
   - ○ second
   - ○ almost

3. Will this ball <u>float</u> in the water?
   - ○ play
   - ○ bounce
   - ● sink

4. Can you <u>remember</u> this short story?
   - ● forget
   - ○ write
   - ○ repeat

5. That clown is very <u>fat</u>!
   - ○ puffy
   - ○ fluffy
   - ● thin

6. Cross this line to <u>start</u> the race.
   - ● finish
   - ○ begin
   - ○ win

7. Get in line and you can <u>follow</u> us.
   - ○ get behind
   - ● lead
   - ○ play with

8. Get to the <u>back</u> of the line!
   - ○ side
   - ● front
   - ○ end

Page 48 — Skill: Antonyms

DIRECTIONS: Read the sentences and answer choices below. Mark the word that means the opposite of the word that is underlined in the sentence.

1. That is a <u>giant</u> teddy bear!
   - ○ big
   - ○ funny
   - ● tiny

2. This was a very <u>hard</u> test!
   - ○ different
   - ● easy
   - ○ bad

3. The book seemed <u>heavy</u> when I carried it.
   - ● light
   - ○ hard
   - ○ easy

4. We must be <u>quiet</u> in this room.
   - ○ happy
   - ○ good
   - ● loud

5. We <u>happily</u> went to the store for mother.
   - ○ joyfully
   - ○ smilingly
   - ● sadly

6. I <u>love</u> to eat pickles with peanut butter.
   - ● hate
   - ○ enjoy
   - ○ don't

7. A <u>huge</u> moth landed on the tree.
   - ○ fuzzy
   - ● small
   - ○ big

8. The birds flew <u>south</u> this morning.
   - ○ east
   - ● north
   - ○ away

Answer Key

Name _____ Skill: Antonyms—Test 9

DIRECTIONS:
Read each of the sentences below. Then, mark the word that means the opposite of the word that is underlined.

1. The windows in the old house were bare.
   - ● covered
   - ○ empty
   - ○ dark

2. Has that camera been broken for very long?
   - ● fixed
   - ○ not working
   - ○ used

3. Is the moon in the sky yet?
   - ● sun
   - ○ star
   - ○ airplane

4. I have a question for you!
   - ○ problem
   - ○ mess
   - ● answer

5. Brian painted a picture of a day in winter.
   - ○ fall
   - ● summer
   - ○ snow

6. It is very cloudy outside today.
   - ○ not right
   - ○ furry
   - ● sunny

7. The child wanted to play with us.
   - ○ baby
   - ● adult
   - ○ boy

8. Andy likes to share all his cookies.
   - ○ give away
   - ● keep
   - ○ eat

Name _____ Skill: Vocabulary

DIRECTIONS:
Read the first part of the sentence and look at the underlined word or words. Choose the word or phrase that means about the same thing as the underlined word. Mark the correct word.

1. To be able to do something means you _____.
   - ○ like to start things
   - ○ are not ready
   - ● can do it

2. To add numbers you _____.
   - ○ take them apart
   - ● put them together
   - ○ put them into groups

3. If I put the lamp against the wall it is _____.
   - ○ far away
   - ● next to
   - ○ on top of

4. The word also means _____.
   - ○ after
   - ○ without
   - ● too

5. When something is above your head it is _____.
   - ○ under
   - ● over
   - ○ beneath

6. To be afraid is to be _____.
   - ● scared
   - ○ angry
   - ○ very happy

7. John is ahead in the race. He is _____.
   - ○ last
   - ○ behind someone
   - ● in front

8. When I get really mad I am _____.
   - ● angry
   - ○ hot
   - ○ shy

Name _____ Skill: Vocabulary—Test 2

DIRECTIONS:
Choose the word that best completes each sentence. Mark the correct word.

1. A word that means not together is _____.
   - ○ with
   - ● apart
   - ○ next to

2. I want to catch a mouse, so I will _____.
   - ○ watch it
   - ○ play with it
   - ● set a trap for it

3. If my glass is empty, then it has _____.
   - ○ something in it
   - ○ a lot in it
   - ● nothing in it

4. If a test is really hard, then it is _____.
   - ○ easy
   - ● difficult
   - ○ fun

5. Another word for under is _____.
   - ● below
   - ○ on
   - ○ beside

6. To collect fire wood is to _____ it.
   - ● gather
   - ○ match
   - ○ trade

7. If Jan follows me in her car, then she will _____.
   - ○ go in front of me
   - ● come behind me
   - ○ not go at all

8. To have a job means you have to _____.
   - ● work
   - ○ go home
   - ○ play

Name _____ Skill: Vocabulary

DIRECTIONS:
Read the first part of the sentence and look at the underlined word or words. Choose the word or phrase that means about the same thing as the underlined word. Mark the correct word.

1. Jim went to the market. He went to the _____.
   - ○ playground
   - ○ school
   - ● store

2. I will not peek at the present. I will not _____.
   - ○ talk
   - ● look
   - ○ move

3. I fell asleep on the way home. I was _____.
   - ○ gone
   - ○ awake
   - ● sleeping

4. A word that means many cows is _____.
   - ● cattle
   - ○ mice
   - ○ cow

5. An ocean is a large _____.
   - ● body of water
   - ○ airplane
   - ○ building

6. A word that means to take something back is _____.
   - ● return
   - ○ borrow
   - ○ give

7. A word that means next to is _____.
   - ○ away
   - ○ below
   - ● beside

8. Mary was upset this morning. She was _____.
   - ● sad
   - ○ pretty
   - ○ glad

Answer Key

Page 53

Skill: Vocabulary

DIRECTIONS: Read the first part of the sentence and look at the underlined word or words. Choose the word or phrase that means about the same thing as the underlined word. Mark the correct word.

1. To enter a room means that you will _____.
   - ○ leave
   - ● go in
   - ○ paint it

2. Work done after school is called _____.
   - ○ play
   - ● homework
   - ○ stuff

3. Another word for message is _____.
   - ● note
   - ○ rub
   - ○ eat

4. To make something perfect is to make it _____.
   - ● right
   - ○ wrong
   - ○ ugly

5. I will always remember you. Always means _____.
   - ○ for three years
   - ○ never
   - ● forever

6. The word join means to _____.
   - ○ take apart
   - ● bring together
   - ○ joke

7. An office is a place where people _____.
   - ○ grow plants
   - ○ live
   - ● work

8. A robber is a _____.
   - ○ friend
   - ○ good person
   - ● thief

Page 54

Skill: Vocabulary

DIRECTIONS: Read the first part of the sentence and look at the underlined word or words. Choose the word or phrase that means about the same thing as the underlined word. Mark the correct word.

1. If you are awake, you are _____.
   - ● not sleeping
   - ○ taking a nap
   - ○ tired

2. If things are not alike, they are _____.
   - ○ together
   - ○ the same
   - ● different

3. To frighten someone is to _____.
   - ○ help
   - ○ share
   - ● scare

4. Another word for woman is _____.
   - ○ girl
   - ○ men
   - ● lady

5. A word that means in the middle is _____.
   - ○ beside
   - ● between
   - ○ after

6. To have everything is to have _____.
   - ● all
   - ○ even
   - ○ until

7. To hope for something is to _____.
   - ○ have
   - ● wish
   - ○ need

8. A neighbor is a someone that _____.
   - ○ teaches
   - ● lives nearby
   - ○ lives far away

Page 55

Skill: Vocabulary

DIRECTIONS: Read the first part of the sentence and look at the underlined word or words. Choose the word or phrase that means about the same thing as the underlined word. Mark the correct word.

1. I go to the zoo often. I have gone _____.
   - ○ a few times
   - ○ once
   - ● many times

2. The bottom part of a plant is the _____.
   - ● root
   - ○ stem
   - ○ leaf

3. A cover that keeps you warm is called a _____.
   - ○ roof
   - ● blanket
   - ○ boot

4. When we dine we _____.
   - ○ read
   - ○ sleep
   - ● eat

5. To have a piece of something is to have _____.
   - ○ a lot
   - ● a part
   - ○ nothing

6. My backyard is the place _____.
   - ○ in front of my house
   - ● behind my house
   - ○ beside my

7. To be certain about something, is to be _____.
   - ○ not sure
   - ● sure
   - ○ upset

8. Another word for trade is _____.
   - ○ buy
   - ● exchange
   - ○ give

Page 56

Skill: Vocabulary

DIRECTIONS: Read the first part of the sentence and look at the underlined word or words. Choose the word or phrase that means about the same thing as the underlined word. Mark the correct word.

1. Another word for middle is _____.
   - ● center
   - ○ back
   - ○ edge

2. A hospital is a place for _____.
   - ○ animals
   - ● people who are sick
   - ○ people who are hungry

3. A part of the body near the head is the _____.
   - ○ finger
   - ○ leg
   - ● neck

4. The word practice means to do something _____.
   - ○ hard
   - ● over and over
   - ○ after awhile

5. A garage is a place to put _____.
   - ○ beds
   - ○ books
   - ● cars

6. Another word for jump is _____.
   - ○ spin
   - ○ walk
   - ● leap

7. To do something once is to do it _____.
   - ● one time
   - ○ two times
   - ○ often

8. When you are in a hurry you _____.
   - ● rush
   - ○ stop
   - ○ crawl

Answer Key

Name _____   Skill: Vocabulary

DIRECTIONS:
Read the first part of the sentence and look at the underlined word or words. Choose the word or phrase that means about the same thing as the underlined word. Mark the correct word.

1. A shelf that is <u>bare</u> has _____.
   - ○ many books
   - ● nothing on it
   - ○ a hole

2. When you <u>chase</u> something you _____.
   - ● run after
   - ○ stay ahead
   - ○ go away

3. Another word for <u>trash</u> is _____.
   - ○ crash
   - ● garbage
   - ○ garage

4. A <u>library</u> is a place to _____.
   - ○ buy food
   - ● borrow books
   - ○ skate

5. When you are <u>not afraid</u> you are _____.
   - ○ hungry
   - ○ scared
   - ● brave

6. To have <u>extra</u> is to have _____.
   - ○ not enough
   - ○ part
   - ● more than enough

7. To <u>sing without words</u> is to _____.
   - ● hum
   - ○ play
   - ○ hang

8. To <u>move the head up and down</u> is to _____.
   - ○ laugh
   - ○ beat
   - ● nod

Name _____   Skill: Vocabulary

DIRECTIONS:
Read the first part of the sentence and look at the underlined word or words. Choose the word or phrase that means about the same thing as the underlined word. Mark the correct word.

1. I <u>own</u> four pets. To own means _____.
   - ○ to feed
   - ● to have
   - ○ to give

2. To <u>scold</u> someone is to _____.
   - ○ burn them
   - ● yell at them
   - ○ be nice to them

3. A <u>fact</u> is something that is _____.
   - ● true
   - ○ not true
   - ○ unreal

4. To <u>track</u> an animal is to _____.
   - ○ scare
   - ● follow
   - ○ look at

5. The word <u>probably</u> means _____.
   - ○ not really
   - ● likely
   - ○ maybe not

6. When I am <u>not wet</u>, I am _____.
   - ● dry
   - ○ damp
   - ○ cold

7. Something that is <u>golden</u> is _____.
   - ○ brown
   - ○ round
   - ● bright yellow

8. A word that means <u>to get together</u> is _____.
   - ○ shop
   - ○ miss
   - ● meet

Name _____   Skill: Vocabulary—Test 10

DIRECTIONS:
Choose the word that best completes each sentence. Mark the correct word.

1. If I beat you in a race, I _____.
   - ○ quit
   - ● win
   - ○ lose

2. When you are early you are _____.
   - ○ on time
   - ○ late
   - ● ahead of time

3. A person that is clever is _____.
   - ● smart
   - ○ dumb
   - ○ sick

4. A word that means not many is _____.
   - ○ plenty
   - ○ lot
   - ● few

5. A breeze is a _____.
   - ○ small bee
   - ○ big cloud
   - ● small wind

6. To build is to _____.
   - ● make
   - ○ take down
   - ○ go in

7. Another word for world is _____.
   - ○ map
   - ● earth
   - ○ state

8. My mom's dad is my _____.
   - ○ uncle
   - ○ cousin
   - ● grandpa

Name _____   Skill: Vocabulary

DIRECTIONS:
Read the first part of the sentence and look at the underlined word or words. Choose the word or phrase that means about the same thing as the underlined word. Mark the correct word.

1. An <u>idea</u> is a _____.
   - ● thought
   - ○ friend
   - ○ kind of game

2. A small <u>part of an hour</u> is _____.
   - ○ a day
   - ○ mine
   - ● a minute

3. The <u>foot of a dog</u> is called the _____.
   - ○ tail
   - ● paw
   - ○ hoof

4. Another name for a <u>heavy blanket</u> is a _____.
   - ● quilt
   - ○ pillow
   - ○ sheet

5. If something is <u>loose</u> it is _____.
   - ○ gone
   - ● not tight
   - ○ small

6. Something that <u>comes in sets of two</u> is a _____.
   - ● pair
   - ○ part
   - ○ point

7. To <u>show that something is right</u> is to _____.
   - ○ pick
   - ○ show
   - ● prove

8. A <u>group of words that go together</u> is a _____.
   - ○ word
   - ● sentence
   - ○ puzzle

Answer Key

Name _____ Skill: Vocabulary—Test 12

DIRECTIONS: Choose the word that best completes each sentence. Mark the correct word.

1. I go before you so I am _____.
   - ○ last
   - ● in front
   - ○ behind

2. To climb a tree is to _____.
   - ● go up
   - ○ get down
   - ○ build in

3. A word that means to cut in two is _____.
   - ○ part
   - ○ chop
   - ● halve

4. A sneaker is a kind of _____.
   - ○ pet
   - ○ game
   - ● shoe

5. Another word for cap is _____.
   - ○ boy
   - ○ raincoat
   - ● hat

6. To be at the end of a line is to be _____.
   - ○ first
   - ○ middle
   - ● last

7. Another word for invite is _____.
   - ○ put together
   - ● ask
   - ○ tell

8. When something is terrible it is very _____.
   - ○ sweet
   - ○ nice
   - ● awful

Name _____ Skill: Vocabulary

DIRECTIONS: Read the first part of the sentence and look at the underlined word or words. Choose the word or phrase that means about the same thing as the underlined word. Mark the correct word.

1. To <u>zoom</u> means to _____.
   - ● move quickly
   - ○ move slowly
   - ○ go by train

2. To <u>close just one eye</u> is to _____.
   - ○ stink
   - ○ blink
   - ● wink

3. To <u>know what something means</u> is to _____.
   - ○ not get
   - ● understand
   - ○ hold

4. The word <u>taste</u> means _____.
   - ○ to feel
   - ○ to wait for
   - ● to take a bite

5. A person who is <u>smart</u> is _____.
   - ○ worn
   - ● wise
   - ○ not bright

6. A word that means <u>to feel</u> is _____.
   - ● touch
   - ○ tap
   - ○ skin

7. The <u>woman a man marries</u> becomes his _____.
   - ○ neighbor
   - ○ daughter
   - ● wife

8. Another word for <u>twig</u> is _____.
   - ● branch
   - ○ bunch
   - ○ tree

Name _____ Skill: Reading Sentences

DIRECTIONS: Read each sentence. Use the picture to help decide which words best complete the story. Mark the space for each answer you have chosen.

We made a tent in my back yard. We used an old

1. blink **blanket** jacket
   ○   ●   ○

and some rope. We tied the rope

2. beside over **between**
   ○   ○   ●

two trees and hung the blanket on it. That night we

3. swam **camped** cramp
   ○   ●   ○

in the tent. It was close to the house so we were not

4. **scared.** angry. glad.
   ●   ○   ○

George went skiing with his father. He wore a hat and

1. **scarf** skate spin
   ●   ○   ○

because it was cold. First, they went to the top of a

2. hall. **mountain.** month.
   ○   ●   ○

George did not know how to ski so he had to take

3. **lessons.** markets. before.
   ●   ○   ○

Then he and his dad went all the way to the

4. behind. **bottom.** moon.
   ○   ●   ○

Name _____ Skill: Reading Sentences

DIRECTIONS: Read each sentence. Use the picture to help decide which words best complete the story. Mark the space for each answer you have chosen.

I like to travel. Last year we went to a different

1. house. room. **country.**
   ○   ○   ●

I saw many new animals. My

2. farther **favorite** finish
   ○   ●   ○

one was the kangaroo. It is a very

3. **strange** wander rich
   ●   ○   ○

animal. Its legs are big and

4. crawl. **strong.** empty.
   ○   ●   ○

Mother bird was looking for a place to

1. block middle **build**
   ○   ○   ●

a nest. She saw a small house on a

2. breeze. **branch.** brook.
   ○   ●   ○

The house was warm and dry. It was a

3. parade pepper **perfect**
   ○   ○   ●

place and would keep her babies

4. third. **safe.** smooth.
   ○   ●   ○

120

Answer Key

Page 65

DIRECTIONS: Read each sentence. Use the picture to help decide which words best complete the story. Mark the space for each answer you have chosen.

Otto is an octopus. He lives in the
1. **ocean** ● camp ○ week ○

Otto is quite large and has eight
2. **legs** ● eyes ○ desks ○

Many people think Otto looks a little
3. deep ○ **scary** ● broke ○

but he is really very
4. fight ○ low ○ **kind** ●

A frog was sitting on a leaf. He was in a
1. penny ○ backyard ○ **pond** ●

He was by himself and wishing for a
2. **friend** ● kitchen ○ hammer ○

to play with. Suddenly he heard a loud
3. **splash** ● spend ○ point ○

A toad had come along. They played together
4. hunter ○ **happily** ● behind ○

Page 66

DIRECTIONS: Read each sentence. Use the picture to help decide which words best complete the story. Mark the space for each answer you have chosen.

Each fall we pick apples. My brother and I
1. cross ○ clip ○ **climb** ●

up the trunk to find the biggest apples. Mother has a
2. **ladder** ● letter ○ listen ○

because she can't reach high
3. edge ○ **enough** ● kept ○

We pick so many apples we can make six
4. throws! ○ plates! ○ **pies!** ●

Sam took a test today. The test was on his
1. shake ○ **spelling** ● soft ○

words. Some of the words were
2. quick ○ whisper ○ **difficult** ●

to spell. Sam did not
3. **study** ● past ○ peek ○

well last night. He was surprised at his poor
4. drop ○ **grade** ● grab ○

Page 67

DIRECTIONS: Read each sentence. Use the picture to help decide which words best complete the story. Mark the space for each answer you have chosen.

I am a tall animal. I am tall because I have a long
1. head ○ **neck** ● nine ○

When I want water, I have to bend my
2. **tail** ● knees ○ knew ○

to reach the ground. I think that I am
3. **lucky** ● lift ○ neither ○

to be so tall. Many of my friends are way too
4. print ○ shade ○ **short** ●

I really like to play outside. Best of all, I like to
1. notice ○ silver ○ **skate** ●

I roll down my sidewalk and out into the
2. **street** ● ship ○ smoke ○

I go very quickly and then stop and
3. splash ○ **spin** ● speak ○

around. In every race, I am always the
4. **winner** ● wander ○ twig ○

Page 68

DIRECTIONS: Read each sentence. Use the picture to help decide which words best complete the story. Mark the space for each answer you have chosen.

Polly is my pet bird. She is a blue and green
1. painter ○ **parrot** ● path ○

Polly talks a lot. She can
2. rest ○ **remember** ● rail ○

many words that she has
3. **locked** ● left ○ learned ○

All of my friends think that Polly is
4. wire ○ **wonderful** ● wheel ○

It was a dark night in the woods. I was a little
1. **afraid** ● alike ○ belong ○

because I did not have a light and the
2. mask ○ **moon** ● junk ○

was behind a cloud. Suddenly I heard a loud
3. **noise!** ● notice! ○ pole! ○

I looked up and saw that it was only a baby
4. quack ○ office ○ **owl** ●

Answer Key

Page 69

Name _____ **Skill: Reading sentences**

DIRECTIONS:
Read each sentence. Use the picture to help decide which words best complete the story. Mark the space for each answer you have chosen.

Once there was a king and queen. They lived in a big

1. circle ○   chase ○   **castle ●**

near the sea. They had a son who was a good

2. mark. ○   price. ○   **prince. ●**

One day he rode to another castle and saw a beautiful

3. **young ●**   year ○   teach ○

girl. They fell in love and got

4. met. ○   **married. ●**   mail. ○

I saw a horse today. It was

1. dive ○   **different ●**   done ○

from any horse I have ever seen! It had black and white

2. salt! ○   slides! ○   **stripes! ●**

I have never seen such a

3. shape ○   sense ○   **strange ●**

horse before. Maybe it was really just a silly

4. drew. ○   **dream. ●**   drum. ○

Page 70

Name _____ **Skill: Reading Sentences**

DIRECTIONS:
Read each of the sentences below. Use the picture to help decide which word best completes the story. Mark the space for each answer you choose.

This is my town. It is a good place to

1. **live. ●**   life. ○   key. ○

My town has a bank and many stores. We have one

2. front ○   **factory ●**   flour ○

where many people work. The farmers grow corn and

3. **cattle. ●**   land. ○   hidden. ○

Nurses and doctors work at our

4. Monday. ○   **hospital. ●**   happen. ○

Kyle likes art. He likes to draw and make

1. whole. ○   **paintings. ●**   mud. ○

He takes his time and will never

2. **rush ●**   rough ○   shine ○

when he paints. He puts different colors on a

3. pass ○   **palette ●**   potato ○

and mixes them together. Kyle is a very good

4. baby. ○   agree. ○   **artist. ●**

Page 71

Name _____ **Skill: Reading Sentences**

DIRECTIONS:
Read each sentence. Use the picture to help decide which words best complete the story. Mark the space for each answer you have chosen.

Amy likes school. Her favorite class is

1. **music. ●**   mirror. ○   learn. ○

Amy can play a

2. five ○   fair ○   **few ●**

songs on her

3. **violin. ●**   vine. ○   voice. ○

But sometimes she breaks a

4. **string! ●**   wing! ○   spent! ○

I like when it begins to rain. The

1. child ○   **clouds ●**   curl ○

gather and it begins to

2. spend. ○   stood. ○   **storm. ●**

I like to hear the rain and the loud

3. taste. ○   **thunder. ●**   toast. ○

When it is over, I can always find the

4. for. ○   **rainbow. ●**   flower. ○

Page 72

Name _____ **Skill: Reading Sentences**

DIRECTIONS:
Read each sentence. Use the picture to help decide which words best complete the story. Mark the space for each answer you have chosen.

I like to watch bees. I am

1. catch ○   **careful ●**   cherry ○

when I am near them because they can

2. **sting. ●**   stare. ○   reach. ○

They live in a large

3. **hive. ●**   horn. ○   gate. ○

That is where they make lots of

4. held. ○   **honey. ●**   hair. ○

Lots of animals live in the woods. This one is a

1. player. ○   owl. ○   **raccoon. ●**

It is a dark color and has a lot of rings on its

2. **tail. ●**   trail. ○   touch. ○

Every raccoon has a

3. march ○   **mask ●**   main ○

around its eyes that makes it look like a

4. river. ○   **robber. ●**   roller! ○

122

Answer Key

Page 73

Name _____ Skill: Reading Sentences

DIRECTIONS: Read each sentence. Use the picture to help decide which words best complete the story. Mark the space for each answer you have chosen.

Jamie has a pet rabbit. Some people call it a

1. **bunny.** ●   honey. ○   knot. ○

Jamie must see that the rabbit gets enough food and

2. drop ○   except ○   **exercise** ●

so it does not get sick. It likes to eat

3. **carrots** ●   coins ○   cattle ○

and other

4. paw. ○   **vegetables.** ●   visit. ○

Pam is so happy! She is going to the

1. circle ○   gate ○   **circus** ●

this week. Some men put up a big

2. **tent** ●   team ○   thumb ○

and brought in lots of

3. worry ○   **wonderful** ●   whole ○

animals. The circus will even have a

4. pipe! ○   **parade!** ●   patch! ○

Page 74

Name _____ Skill: Reading Sentences

DIRECTIONS: Read each sentence. Use the picture to help decide which words best complete the story. Mark the space for each answer you have chosen.

Thanksgiving is almost here! It is my

1. fair ○   good ○   **favorite** ●

day of the year. I like to

2. drink ○   **taste** ●   thin ○

all the good foods. We always have

3. **turkey.** ●   toad. ○   spill. ○

At the end of the meal we eat pumpkin

4. paste. ○   **pie.** ●   pile. ○

Let's play ball! We can play

1. oven. ○   **outside.** ●   order. ○

First, I will

2. sweet ○   though ○   **throw** ●

the ball to you. Then you can

3. cross ○   **catch** ●   caught ○

it and toss it back. If you can't throw well, I will not

4. **mind.** ●   mile. ○   map. ○

Page 75

Name _____ Skill: Reading Sentences

DIRECTIONS: Read each sentence. Use the picture to help decide which words best complete the story. Mark the space for each answer you have chosen.

The sky is fun to watch at night. In the

1. sunlight ○   **summer** ●   sank ○

the stars are easy to see. They are

2. **shiny** ●   size ○   seven ○

bits of white light way up there. The man on the

3. meow ○   himself ○   **moon** ●

looks like he wants to

4. **wink!** ●   bunch! ○   east! ○

I drew a picture of my house. The window in the

1. fear ○   **front** ●   clear ○

is the one in my

2. dust. ○   **bedroom.** ●   garden. ○

The house next door looks just like mine. My

3. net ○   neither ○   **neighbor** ●

is nice. Each morning she brings us the

4. neck. ○   **newspaper.** ●   mark. ○

Page 76

Name _____ Skill: Narrative Passages

DIRECTIONS: Read each story then, read each question. For each question mark the space for the answer you think is right. Write the answer for number five on a separate piece of paper.

Cookies are my favorite treat. I eat them every day after school. I have a glass of milk with them. My mother makes fresh cookies just before I get home.

1. What do I like to eat?
   cookies ●   chips ○   meat ○

2. What do I drink?
   water ○   **milk** ●   juice ○

3. How do the cookies feel?
   cold ○   hard ○   **warm** ●

4. Why does mother make cookies each day?
   ○ she hates to cook
   ● she knows I like them
   ○ she eats them all

5. What is your favorite treat for after school?

Halley is my best friend. She lives next door to me. We see each other every day. We both like to draw and collect rocks.

1. My best friend is
   Halley ●   Drew ○   Nancy ○

2. We like to find
   days ○   friends ○   **rocks** ●

3. Halley is my
   neighbor ●   cousin ○   sister ○

4. A good name for this story is
   ○ Playing Together
   ○ Collecting Rocks
   ● My Best Friend

5. Why do you think Halley and I are such good friends?

Answer Key

Name _____
Skill: Narrative Passages

DIRECTIONS:
Read each story then, read each question. For each question mark the space for the answer you think is right. Write the answer for number five on a separate piece of paper.

In the fall, the leaves on the trees change colors. They turn yellow and red then drop to the ground. I like to play in them, but I don't like to rake them!

1. When do leaves change?
   - summer ○
   - fall ●
   - winter ○

2. I like to _____ leaves.
   - burn ○
   - play in ●
   - rake ○

3. After leaves change, they
   - fall ●
   - grow ○
   - change ○

4. I don't like to rake leaves because it is
   - ○ different
   - ● hard work
   - ○ lots of fun

5. How are you like the person in this story?

Mike is the best bike rider on his block. He can go fast and wins every race. He can stop quickly and spin around in a circle. He can even ride without using his hands!

1. What does Mike ride?
   - horses ○
   - circles ○
   - a bike ●

2. He can ride with no
   - feet ○
   - hands ●
   - blocks ○

3. In a race, Mike is always the
   - winner ●
   - loser ○
   - slowest ○

4. Mike is so good because he has probably
   - ○ ridden a skate board
   - ○ had many bikes
   - ● practiced a lot

5. Why does Mike need to be careful riding with no hands?

Name _____
Skill: Narrative Passages

DIRECTIONS:
Read each story then, read each question. For each question mark the space for the answer you think is right. Write the answer for number five on a separate piece of paper.

Sometimes it is best to be slow. When you are doing work that needs to be done carefully, you should take your time. Being the fastest is not always being the best!

1. The story is about being
   - best ○
   - slow ●
   - quick ○

2. Fast is not always
   - time ○
   - bad ○
   - best ●

3. Go slow when you must be
   - careful ●
   - quick ○
   - first ○

4. A good name for this story might be
   - ○ Faster is Better
   - ● Slow and Careful
   - ○ The Slow Snail

5. Name a job or time when you need to be slow.

Mom just had a new baby. I do not have any fun with him. He sleeps all day and can't play yet. Mom spends a lot of time with him.

1. Mom had a
   - girl ○
   - nap ○
   - baby ●

2. What does he do all day?
   - play ○
   - eat ○
   - sleep ●

3. The new baby is my
   - brother ●
   - sister ○
   - pal ○

4. How do I feel about the baby?
   - ● I don't like him much
   - ○ I like to hold him
   - ○ We are good friends

5. How might I change my feelings about the baby?

Name _____
Skill: Narrative Passages

DIRECTIONS:
Read each story then, read each question. For each question mark the space for the answer you think is right. Write the answer for number five on a separate piece of paper.

There is a treehouse in the back yard. Do you want to play there? It has a rope to swing from. We can pretend to be anything we like. No one will find us up there.

1. I want to play in a
   - tree ○
   - treehouse ●
   - yard ○

2. What is in the treehouse?
   - a chair ○
   - a rope ●
   - a swing ○

3. Why do I like the treehouse?
   - it is tall ○
   - it is scary ○
   - it is fun ●

4. Why won't anyone find us up there?
   - ○ everyone is sleeping
   - ● the leaves hide us
   - ○ we are invisible

5. What games would you play in a treehouse?

Alyssa takes dancing lessons. She has learned to move and spin with the music. She listens carefully and does what the teacher says. Alyssa would like to be a dancer when she grows up.

1. Who is the girl in the story?
   - Mary ○
   - teacher ○
   - Alyssa ●

2. She learns by taking
   - lessons ●
   - music ○
   - dancer ○

3. Alyssa _____ dancing.
   - hates ○
   - enjoys ●
   - stopped ○

4. What tells you how Alyssa feels about dancing? She
   - ○ learned to spin
   - ○ takes lessons
   - ● wants to be a dancer

5. What kind of dance do you think Alyssa is learning?

Name _____
Skill: Narrative Passages

DIRECTIONS:
Read each story then, read each question. For each question mark the space for the answer you think is right. Write the answer for number five on a separate piece of paper.

Puppies are funny. They chase balls and growl at shoes. They run in circles, chasing their tails. Puppies lick your face and make you laugh.

1. This story is about
   - playing ○
   - tails ○
   - puppies ●

2. Puppies like to chase
   - shoes ○
   - balls ●
   - faces ○

3. Puppies are fun to
   - play with ●
   - feed ○
   - look at ○

4. The person telling this story
   - ○ has a puppy
   - ● likes puppies
   - ○ laughs a lot

5. What is the hard part about raising a puppy?

Crossing the street is not easy! First you must stop at the corner. Look both ways because a car could come from around a corner. Look once more before you cross.

1. This story is about crossing
   - corners ○
   - yards ○
   - streets ●

2. Stop at the corner
   - never ○
   - first ●
   - second ○

3. Crossing the street can be
   - difficult ●
   - fun ○
   - easy ○

4. Why should you look two times?
   - ● a car may be coming
   - ○ so the car will see you
   - ○ just because

5. Tell about crossing a street when it is not safe.

Answer Key

Name _____ Skill: Narrative Passages

DIRECTIONS:
Read each story then, read each question. For each question mark the space for the answer you think is right. Write the answer for number five on a separate piece of paper.

Friday is my favorite day. Mom picks me up from school and we go rent a movie. We go home and I can play until dark. Then, I come home and we order a pizza and watch the movie!

1. What day is my favorite?

Tuesday	Monday	Friday
○	○	●

2. What do we rent?

a movie	a pizza	games
●	○	○

3. I probably don't have

homework	dinner	a pet
●	○	○

4. Why can I play so late on Fridays?
- ○ my mom is mean
- ○ it is pizza night
- ● no school the next day

5. What is your favorite thing to do on Friday? Why?

I don't like being so small. I can't reach high shelves or see over fences. I have to ask for help all the time. One good thing is that I can hide better than any of my friends!

1. I am not happy with being

tall	small	young
○	●	○

2. I always seem to need

shelves	help	time
○	●	○

3. I hide better because I am

smart	older	small
○	○	●

4. A good name for this story might be
- ● I Am Small
- ○ Tall People
- ○ Good Hiding Places

5. In what other ways is it good to be small?

Name _____ Skill: Narrative Passages

DIRECTIONS:
Read each story then, read each question. For each question mark the space for the answer you think is right. Write the answer for number five on a separate piece of paper.

Roger has a rock collection. He takes long walks in the mountains and picks up rocks that he sees. Some rocks are as big as a box. Others are so tiny you can hardly see them!

1. Who collects rocks?

Roger	boxes	Father
●	○	○

2. He found his rocks in the

ocean	mountains	sand
○	●	○

3. Roger must like to

run	walk	eat
○	●	○

4. Roger looks for rocks in the mountains because
- ○ he likes to climb
- ● many rocks are there
- ○ it is cooler

5. What is an easy thing to collect? Why?

It is the time of year when the pond is starting to burst with life. Fish are laying eggs. Butterflies are on all the flowers. The water is fresh and clear. Frogs croak and sing all night.

1. What croaks at night?

frogs	flowers	fish
●	○	○

2. What are laying eggs?

frogs	butterflies	fish
○	○	●

3. Life at the pond is

lonely	ugly	happy
○	○	●

4. What time of year is it?
- ○ fall
- ○ winter
- ● spring

5. What is your favorite time of year? Why?

Name _____ Skill: Narrative Passages

DIRECTIONS:
Read each story. Then, read each question and mark the space for the answer you think is right. Write your answer for number five on a separate sheet of paper.

David has a box of magic tricks. He does tricks for his friends. David wears a tall hat and black cape. He waves a wand and pulls a rabbit from his hat. His friends ask him to do it again.

1. David wears a black

hat	cape	wand
○	●	○

2. What comes from the hat?

rabbit	magic	wand
●	○	○

3. David wants to be a

student	magician	friend
○	●	○

4. What do David's friends think about his trick?
- ○ they don't care
- ● they really like it
- ○ they are scared

5. Which is better, the rabbit trick or a disappearing coin?

I went to the store with Dad. I stopped to look at a great toy. When I looked up, Dad was gone. He was lost! I was a little scared so I called his name. Dad came around the corner and smiled.

1. We were at the

school	store	bank
○	●	○

2. What made me stop?

Dad	a toy	a man
○	●	○

3. Who was really lost?

Dad	me	you
○	●	○

4. Why was Dad gone?
- ○ he went to get eat lunch
- ○ he stopped to look
- ● he didn't know I stopped

5. Who was lost, Dad or me? Why?

Name _____ Skill: Narrative Passages

DIRECTIONS:
Read each story then, read each question. For each question mark the space for the answer you think is right. Write the answer for number five on a separate piece of paper.

There is a new girl at my school. Her name is Nancy and she smiles a lot. She sits behind me but doesn't say much. I wonder what she likes to do for fun. Maybe I will ask her to play with me.

1. The new girl's name is

Mimi	Natalie	Nancy
○	○	●

2. She sits _____ me.

next to	behind	beside
○	●	○

3. Nancy is probably

mean	shy	angry
○	●	○

4. Nancy is probably quiet because she
- ● is a little scared
- ○ doesn't like children
- ○ wants to eat lunch

5. What can you do to help a new student at school?

I ate an apple and put the seeds in a cup. I put water on the seeds and left them alone for one week. I put the seeds into a pot of dirt. With lots of water and sun, it might grow!

1. What did I eat?

pear	peach	apple
○	○	●

2. First, I put the seeds in

a cup	water	dirt
●	○	○

3. I left the seeds in water for

3 days	7 days	8 days
○	●	○

4. If the seeds grow, they will become
- ○ a giant tree
- ○ an oak tree
- ● an apple tree

5. What is the best kind of plant to grow indoors?

Answer Key

Name _____
Skill: Narrative Passages

DIRECTIONS:
Read each story then, read each question. For each question mark the space for the answer you think is right. Write the answer for number five on a separate piece of paper.

Mother says I have to shine my shoes. They are dusty and have a little mud on the bottom. Mother says I cannot go if my shoes are dirty. I like them just the way they are.

1. My shoes are

    old   **dusty**   smelly
    ○   ●   ○

2. If I don't shine them I can't

    eat   run   **go**
    ○   ○   ●

3. My shoes do not look

    clean   used   black
    ●   ○   ○

4. Mother wants them to look nice because
    - ○ she likes dirty shoes
    - ○ she wants new shoes
    - ● they will look better

5. Do you think I should shine my shoes? Why?

It was a day in July. James had been playing in the yard. He wanted something cold to drink. He got the hose and turned it on. Splash! Water hit him right in the face!

1. What was James doing?

    skating   running   **playing**
    ○   ○   ●

2. James wanted a cold

    hose   **drink**   day
    ○   ●   ○

3. It was probably a ___ day.

    cool   **hot**   rainy
    ○   ●   ○

4. How did James feel? He was probably
    - ○ angry at the hose
    - ● happy to cool off
    - ○ sad to waste water

5. What should James do now that he is so wet?

Name _____
Skill: Narrative Passages

DIRECTIONS:
Read each story then, read each question. For each question mark the space for the answer you think is right. Write the answer for number five on a separate piece of paper.

Today has been a terrible day. I banged my knee on the bed. I lost one of my good shoes and had to wear an old pair. In the spelling bee, I lost right away. What else can go wrong?

1. What kind of day was it?

    terrible   wonderful   nice
    ●   ○   ○

2. I hurt my

    shoe   head   **knee**
    ○   ○   ●

3. How do I feel about today?

    happy   excited   **angry**
    ○   ○   ●

4. Where did this story take place?
    - ○ in the backyard
    - ● at home and school
    - ○ at the store

5. What can I do to make it a better day?

Ted is a taxi. He picks up people and takes them to different places. He likes his job. He gets to meet many nice people. He gets to see everything in the city. Ted is a happy taxi.

1. The taxi's name is

    Joe   people   **Ted**
    ○   ○   ●

2. The taxi takes people

    to work   home   **places**
    ○   ○   ●

3. Ted cannot go

    in rivers   home   to work
    ●   ○   ○

4. Ted likes his job because he
    - ● likes to see things
    - ○ hates to travel
    - ○ wants to be a person

5. What makes a job good?

Name _____
Skill: Expository Passages

DIRECTIONS:
Read each story. Then, read each question or statement and mark the space for the answer you think is right. Write your answer for number five on a separate sheet of paper.

People live together in towns or cities. They help each other by the jobs they do. A place where people live and work together is called a community.

1. People help each other by having different

    towns   **jobs**   cities
    ○   ●   ○

2. A town or city is where people live and work

    together   for fun   apart
    ●   ○   ○

3. Which place is not a community for people?

    town   village   **river**
    ○   ○   ●

4. People help each other because we cannot
    - ● do everything alone
    - ○ have friends
    - ○ live alone

5. What jobs do you think help people the most?

Police officers are people who help in your community. Their job is to see that people obey the laws that keep us safe. Police watch over our roads, neighborhoods and stores.

1. Who watches over our community?

    police   laws   stores
    ●   ○   ○

2. Police officers make sure all people obey our

    job   roads   **laws**
    ○   ○   ●

3. It is good to have police around because they

    laugh a lot   **protect us**   are cute
    ○   ●   ○

4. The police are people that
    - ○ chase us
    - ● help a community
    - ○ put out fires

5. Why do the police give tickets for speeding?

Name _____
Skill: Expository Passages

DIRECTIONS:
Read each story. Then, read each question or statement and mark the space for the answer you think is right. Write your answer for number five on a separate sheet of paper.

Who helps when a building catches on fire? Firefighters do. They bring large trucks with long hoses. They go into burning homes to save people who are still inside. They fight fires with water.

1. Who puts out fires?

    police   teachers   **firefighters**
    ○   ○   ●

2. What is used to put out fires?

    trucks   ladders   **water**
    ○   ○   ●

3. A firefighter's job is

    easy   fun   **dangerous**
    ○   ○   ●

4. Firefighters help keep us
    - ○ from getting sick
    - ● safe
    - ○ from breaking laws

5. Would you like to be a firefighter? Why or why not?

Doctors are people who help others. We go to a doctor when we are sick or hurt. Doctors find what is wrong and give us medicine or fix broken bones. We need doctors in our community.

1. Doctors can help us when we are

    sick   tired   old
    ●   ○   ○

2. A doctor might give us

    a cold   **medicine**   a bone
    ○   ●   ○

3. Doctors can also help keep us

    young   rich   **healthy**
    ○   ○   ●

4. You would go to a doctor if you
    - ○ had a broken TV
    - ○ ate dinner
    - ● broke your leg

5. What does your doctor do to help you?

Answer Key

Page 89

Skill: Expository Passages

DIRECTIONS:
Read each story. Then, read each question or statement and mark the space for the answer you think is right. Write your answer for number five on a separate sheet of paper.

When you have a sore tooth you go to a dentist. Dentists live in our community. They help keep our teeth clean and healthy. They can fix a chipped tooth or fill a cavity.

1. What is this story about?
   - ● dentists
   - ○ teeth
   - ○ cleaning

2. Dentists help us keep our teeth
   - ○ chipped
   - ● healthy
   - ○ sore

3. A dentist helps us take care of our
   - ○ hair
   - ○ body
   - ● mouth

4. A dentist can
   - ○ fix a broken arm
   - ● fill a cavity
   - ○ give out speeding tickets

5. Describe what it is like when you visit the dentist.

Farmers are part of our community. They grow many of the foods we eat. Farmers raise animals that are used for food and clothing. We need farmers so we have good things to eat.

1. Farmers help communities by growing
   - ○ cows
   - ○ tomatoes
   - ● food

2. Animals can be used for clothing and
   - ○ pets
   - ● food
   - ○ jobs

3. Without farmers, many people would be
   - ● hungry
   - ○ old
   - ○ fat

4. Farmers are a part of our
   - ○ cars
   - ● communities
   - ○ corn

5. How did a farmer help you today?

Page 90

Skill: Expository Passages

DIRECTIONS:
Read each story then read each question. Read all the answers then mark the space for the answer you think is best. Write the answer for number five on the back of this paper.

Store keepers provide many things that people need. They bring different "goods" to one place where we can shop. Without store keepers, we would have to go many places to buy what we need.

1. This story is about people who own
   - ○ goods
   - ● stores
   - ○ needs

2. Store keepers bring many goods to one
   - ● place
   - ○ house
   - ○ truck

3. Store keepers bring together many things we
   - ○ have
   - ● need
   - ○ hate

4. As used in the story, the word "goods" means
   - ● things to buy
   - ○ food
   - ○ stores

5. We can make clothes. Why do we buy them from stores?

Neighbors are the people who live near you. You see these people almost every day. Neighbors help each other in many ways. They talk to each other and watch over the neighborhood.

1. People who live near you are
   - ● neighbors
   - ○ friends
   - ○ strangers

2. You probably see your neighbor at least once a
   - ○ year
   - ○ month
   - ● day

3. A neighbor who helps you is like a
   - ○ teacher
   - ● friend
   - ○ doctor

4. A good neighbor might do this when you are away
   - ○ have a big party
   - ○ do nothing
   - ● watch your house

5. What have you done to help your neighbor?

Page 91

Skill: Expository Passages

DIRECTIONS:
Read each story then read each question. Read all the answers then mark the space for the answer you think is best. Write the answer for number five on the back of this paper.

When we are hungry but do not want to cook, we can go to a restaurant. We can sit down and wait while the food is cooked then brought to the table. We do not all have to eat the same thing.

1. We can go to a restaurant if we don't want to
   - ○ sit down
   - ● cook
   - ○ eat

2. In some restaurants, you sit and wait at a
   - ● table
   - ○ stove
   - ○ hungry

3. A restaurant is a place where we can buy
   - ● meals
   - ○ groceries
   - ○ water

4. Something you could not order at a restaurant is
   - ○ cheese
   - ● books
   - ○ meat

5. Where is your favorite place to eat? Why?

Every community has a school. Teachers help us learn many new things. Together we read, write and do math every day. We need to learn these things to get a good job.

1. Children go to school to
   - ○ hide
   - ○ write
   - ● learn

2. Who helps us at school?
   - ○ uncles
   - ● teachers
   - ○ sisters

3. What does learning help us get when we are older?
   - ● jobs
   - ○ birds
   - ○ new things

4. Which is something we might learn at school?
   - ○ how to cut logs
   - ● how to count by tens
   - ○ how to sleep

5. What subject do you like best? Why?

Page 92

Skill: Expository Passages

DIRECTIONS:
Read each story then read each question. Read all the answers then mark the space for the answer you think is best. Write the answer for number five on the back of this paper.

Want to read a book? Go to the library! There are many books and tapes there for you to borrow. You must bring them back in a week or two so other people can use them, too.

1. What can you borrow from a library?
   - ○ shoes
   - ● books
   - ○ furniture

2. You can keep the books or tapes for one or two
   - ● weeks
   - ○ months
   - ○ years

3. Each book you borrow from the library costs
   - ○ 50 cents
   - ○ a dollar
   - ● nothing

4. The library is a good place to
   - ○ see a play
   - ● study and find facts
   - ○ watch a parade

5. What is the best book you ever read? Why was it good?

A hospital is a place we go if we are very sick or hurt. Doctors and nurses work there. They watch over you day and night. They give you medicine that helps to make you healthy again.

1. Who does not work in a hospital?
   - ○ nurse
   - ● waitress
   - ○ doctor

2. What do nurses bring to make you well?
   - ○ food
   - ○ candy
   - ● medicine

3. In a hospital you are always
   - ○ alone
   - ● watched
   - ○ hot

4. You should go to a hospital when you have
   - ○ a head ache
   - ○ a cold
   - ● a bad cut

5. Would you like to work in a hospital? Why or why not?

Answer Key

Name _____
Skill: Expository Passages

DIRECTIONS:
Read each story then read each question. Read all the answers then mark the space for the answer you think is best. Write the answer for number five on the back of this paper.

Your body has many parts. The outside is covered with skin that lets you feel things. You have arms and legs to help you move. You have eyes for seeing and ears for hearing.

1. With which part of the body do we see?

    ears ○   eyes ●   arms ○

2. What covers the outside of the body?

    legs ○   arms ○   skin ●

3. When you are tickled you

    feel it ●   hear it ○   smell it ○

4. Our arms and legs
    ○ have a shell covering
    ● help us to go
    ○ help us to hear things

5. Which part of the body do you think is most important?

The heart is an organ inside your chest. It is about as big as your fist. The heart pumps blood to every part of your body. The blood carries things your body needs to work and grow.

1. The organ inside the chest is called the

    heart ●   blood ○   body ○

2. What does the heart pump?

    fist ○   blood ●   chest ○

3. What might the blood carry to our body parts?

    food ●   anger ○   plants ○

4. Your heart does not ever
    ○ beat fast
    ○ help your body
    ● take a rest

5. What can you do to keep your heart healthy?

Name _____
Skill: Expository Passages

DIRECTIONS:
Read each story. Then, read each question or statement and mark the space for the answer you think is right. Write your answer for number five on a separate sheet of paper.

There are two lungs inside the chest. Lungs bring air from the nose into the body. The air passes from the lungs into the blood where it is taken to other parts of the body. We need air to live.

1. How many lungs do we have?

    three ○   two ●   one ○

2. Where does air come into the body? Through the

    nose ●   eyes ○   ears ○

3. If we had no lungs, our bodies could not get

    food ○   water ○   air ●

4. Why does your chest get bigger when you inhale?
    ○ the lungs get smaller
    ● it fills with air
    ○ it pushes out air

5. Is it better to breathe slowly or quickly? Why?

Food we eat passes from the mouth to the stomach. The food is too big to be used by the body so the stomach breaks the food into tiny bits. The blood carries these bits to other parts of the body.

1. What carries food to other parts of the body?

    mouth ○   stomach ○   blood ●

2. Which body part touches the food first?

    stomach ○   blood ○   mouth ●

3. The stomach helps us by making our food

    tasty ○   warmer ○   smaller ●

4. Why does the stomach break down food into bits?
    ○ it looks better like that
    ○ it helps you grow
    ● to help the body use it

5. Is pizza a good food for our body? Why or why not?

Name _____
Skill: Expository Passages

DIRECTIONS:
Read each story then read each question. Read all the answers then mark the space for the answer you think is best. Write the answer for number five on the back of this paper.

The brain is an organ inside the head. It tells your body what to do. You do not tell your heart to pump or lungs to breathe. Your brain does! It tells you what your eyes see and your skin feels.

1. Which organ is found in the head?

    heart ○   brain ●   lungs ○

2. The brain tells your heart to

    pump ●   breathe ○   see ○

3. Of all the body parts the brain is probably the most

    useless ○   important ●   unlucky ○

4. Which does your brain control without your help?
    ○ chewing food
    ○ reading
    ● getting air to the body

5. What do you think is the most important organ? Why?

Each part of your body has an important job to do. All the body parts work together to help you move, feel, see and think. Working together, the body parts keep you alive and well.

1. Each body part is

    seeing ○   together ○   important ●

2. The parts of the body work

    together ●   apart ○   alive ○

3. Working together, body parts help keep you

    lucky ○   alive ●   dead ○

4. This story is about
    ○ spare parts
    ○ car parts
    ● body parts

5. What might happen if one body part doesn't work?

Name _____
Skill: Expository Passages

DIRECTIONS:
Read each story then read each question. Read all the answers then mark the space for the answer you think is best. Write the answer for number five on the back of this paper.

Do you take care of your body? Good food, lots of water, exercise, and rest can help your body stay strong and healthy. You must take care of your body so it can take care of you!

1. This story is about taking care of your

    body ●   food ○   hair ○

2. One thing your body needs is

    heat ○   rest ●   candy ○

3. Taking good care of your body is

    needless ○   smart ●   silly ○

4. When you don't take care of your body, you might
    ● get sick
    ○ grow taller
    ○ win a race

5. What do you do to take care of your body everyday?

Muscles need to be used if you want them to stay strong. Exercise is one way to use your muscles. Running, riding bikes, skating, playing, and walking are all good ways to exercise your muscles.

1. What do your muscles need?

    water ○   sun ○   exercise ●

2. Exercise will keep your muscles

    soft ○   strong ●   easy ○

3. If your do not use your muscles, they will become

    weak ●   strong ○   bigger ○

4. Running, skating, and walking are good ways to
    ○ rest
    ○ take a bath
    ● exercise

5. What is your favorite way to exercise? Why?

Answer Key

Name _____ Skill: Expository Passages

DIRECTIONS:
Read each story then read each question. Read all the answers then mark the space for the answer you think is best. Write the answer for number five on the back of this paper.

Does washing your hands help your body? Yes! Every day your hands pick up germs, tiny living things you can't see. Germs can make you sick. Washing your hands gets rid of most germs.

1. Tiny living things that you can't see are
   - **germs** ●   worms ○   hands ○

2. We get germs on our hands every
   - **day** ●   week ○   month ○

3. Washing your hands helps keep you
   - sick ○   **healthy** ●   sleepy ○

4. What is the main idea of this story?
   - ○ germs are bad
   - ● keep your hands clean
   - ○ take a bath

5. How often should you wash your hands each day?

The clothes you wear can help keep your body healthy. You need to stay warm enough and dry. The clothes you wear can keep you warm or cool. They can also keep you dry in the rain!

1. Our bodies must stay dry and
   - hot ○   wet ○   **warm** ●

2. Wearing clothes helps to keep our body
   - **healthy** ●   clean ○   cold ○

3. What could you use to keep your body dry?
   - sweater ○   **umbrella** ●   swim suit ○

4. What should you do if you get cold and wet?
   - ○ put on boots
   - ○ drink something cool
   - ● put on dry clothes

5. What is the best way to stay cool in the summer?

Name _____ Skill: Expository Passages

DIRECTIONS:
Read each story. Then, read each question or statement and mark the space for the answer you think is right. Write your answer for number five on a separate sheet of paper.

Teeth are important. Without them, we can not eat many of the foods our bodies need. Keep your teeth clean by brushing after every meal. Have a dentist look at them two times every year.

1. This story is about
   - dentists ○   foods ○   **teeth** ●

2. How many times a year should you see the dentist?
   - **two** ●   three ○   five ○

3. How many times a day should you brush?
   - one ○   two ○   **three** ●

4. Without teeth we could not
   - ○ go to school
   - ● eat many types of food
   - ○ walk

5. What is the best thing to do for healthy teeth?

When you get sick, you might take medicine to make you well. It can be a shot, pills, or a drink. Some medicines keep us from catching an illness. Medicines can help us stay healthy.

1. We take medicine when we are
   - sleepy ○   old ○   **sick** ●

2. You can take medicine as a drink, a shot, or a
   - **pill** ●   toy ○   meal ○

3. Medicine helps us feel
   - **better** ●   hot ○   sick ○

4. What is not a type of medicine?
   - ● mumps
   - ○ pills
   - ○ a shot

5. What kind of medicine do you like to take? Why?

Name _____ Skill: Letters

DIRECTIONS:
Read each letter then read each question about the letter. Decide which is the best answer to the question. Mark the space for the answer you have chosen. Write the answer to number four on a separate piece of paper.

> July 16
> Dear Peg,
>   My scout troop is having a picnic at the lake next Tuesday. We will play games, sing songs, and swim before we eat. We will have a big fire and cook our hotdogs over it. Would you like to come with me?
>   Your friend,
>   Sandy

1. Who is this letter for?
   - **Peg** ●   Sandy ○   scouts ○

2. What day is the picnic?
   - July ○   **Tuesday** ●   Friday ○

3. What time of year is it?
   - spring ○   **summer** ●   fall ○

4. What other things might scouts to do together?

> August 6
> Dear Lyle,
>   I went on vacation with my family for three weeks. We camped in Yellowstone Park and saw many wild animals. A bear tried to get into our food box! Mom and I got into the car, but dad was in the tent. We were glad when he left!
>   Love,
>   Peter

1. Who wrote this?
   - Lyle ○   **Peter** ●   Mom ○

2. What is Yellowstone?
   - bear ○   **park** ●   vacation ○

3. How did Peter feel when the bear came?
   - happy ○   **scared** ●   mad ○

4. Would you go camping on your vacation? Why?

Name _____ Skill: Letters

DIRECTIONS:
Read each letter then read each question about the letter. Decide which is the best answer to the question. Mark the space for the answer you have chosen. Write the answer to number four on a separate piece of paper.

> September 8
> Dear Mr. White,
>   I did not mean to break your window. We were playing ball and I hit a home run over the fence. I did not know it would hit your house. I will pay to have the window fixed. I will be more careful next time.
>   Sincerely,
>   Frank

1. What was Frank playing?
   - **baseball** ●   tennis ○   soccer ○

2. What was broken?
   - fence ○   house ○   **window** ●

3. What is Frank trying to tell Mr. White? He is
   - **sorry** ●   glad ○   angry ○

4. What do you think Mr. White might say to Frank?

> November 16
> Dear Aunt Alice,
>   Can you come to our house for Thanksgiving this year? We have a huge turkey and mom is making your favorite pie. We can watch the parades and eat all day! You can even bring your dog, Max, if you like.
>   Your niece,
>   Helen

1. Who wrote this letter?
   - Alice ○   Max ○   **Helen** ●

2. Thanksgiving is a
   - week ○   **holiday** ●   parade ○

3. Helen wrote this letter to Aunt Alice to say
   - miss you ○   thank you ○   **please come** ●

4. What do you think is Aunt Alice's favorite pie? Why?

Answer Key

Page 101

Skill: Letters

DIRECTIONS: Read each letter then read each question about the letter. Decide which is the best answer to the question. Mark the space for the answer you have chosen. Write the answer to number four on a separate piece of paper.

January 4
Dear Bob,
  I really like the present you gave me. I take very good care of him. I named him Fangs because he chews on everything. Fangs sleeps next to my bed at night. He purrs when I rub his ears. He is the best pet ever!
    Sincerely,
    Nick

1. Who gave the present?
   Nick Fangs **Bob**

2. What does Fangs like to do?
   eat sleep **chew**

3. What kind of pet is Fangs?
   dog horse **cat**

4. Is a pet a good gift to give? Why or why not?

March 27
Dear Mr. Broom,
  Joey does not have his work ready for school today. He had just started to do it last night when a monster knocked at our door. Joey let him in and the monster ate every bit of paper in the house! Joey will have it done tomorrow.
    Sincerely,
    Joey's Mom

1. When will Joey have his homework finished?
   next week Friday **tomorrow**

2. Who took the homework?
   Mr. Broom Joey **a monster**

3. Who is Mr. Broom?
   coach **teacher** father

4. Do you think Joey's mom really wrote this letter?

Page 102

Skill: Letters

May 5
Dear Mom,
  I picked these flowers just for you. There are roses and tulips from our garden. I know you don't want me to cut your flowers, but I wanted you to know how much I love you! Please don't be angry with me.
    Love,
    Cindy

1. What month is it?
   March **May** August

2. What flowers didn't Cindy pick?
   roses **daisies** tulips

3. Cindy wanted to tell mom that she
   is pretty is sorry **loves her**

4. How will mother feel about Cindy picking the flowers?

July 17
Dear Phil,
  I think I left my robot at your house when I spent the night. We were playing with it in the treehouse when your mom called us for dinner. Would you please see if it is still there? I really would like to have it back.
    Your buddy,
    Mel

1. What did Mel lose?
   robot dinner a shoe

2. Where should Phil look for the toy?
   treehouse school bedroom

3. What time of year is it?
   summer winter fall

4. What should Phil do if the robot isn't in the treehouse?

Page 103

Skill: Letters

September 2
Dear Susan,
  Don't forget to look at the stars tonight. You will be able to see a comet in the north part of the sky. It will be very bright and have two tails! We won't see this comet again for another hundred years.
    Look up!
    Mary

1. To whom is this letter written?
   Susan Mary comet

2. Mary is telling Susan to look for a
   star **comet** year

3. This comet is not seen
   tonight **often** ever

4. Is it fun to look at the stars? Why or why not?

December 8
Dear Grandma,
  Thank you for taking me shopping today. I found a gift for everyone on my list! It was lots of fun to talk with you while we looked in the stores. I really enjoyed the lunch we shared, too. Let's do it again soon.
    Love,
    Linda

1. What did Grandma and Linda do?
   play **shop** dance

2. Linda wrote this letter to tell grandma
   thank you hello write

3. What were they shopping for?
   shoes **presents** a list

4. Where would you like to go with your grandma?

Page 104

Skill: Letters

February 29
Dear Elmer,
  There is something very special about this day. Do you know what it is? This day only happens every four years. It is an extra day in February! This year is called Leap Year.
    Your pal,
    R.J.

1. Who wrote this letter?
   Elmer **R.J.** February

2. This special day comes once every
   year 2 years **4 years**

3. How many days are usually in February?
   7 **28** 29

4. Which day of the year is your favorite? Why?

April 25
Dear Julie,
  I am having a party next Tuesday. Can you come? There will be colored balloons, cake, ice cream, and games. I will put eight candles on the cake, make a wish, then blow them out. Do you know what kind of party it is?
    Please come,
    Betty

1. Betty asking Julie to come to
   school a boat **a party**

2. When does Betty want her to come?
   today **Tuesday** Saturday

3. What kind of party is it?
   dance **birthday** surprise

4. What is the most fun thing to do at a party?

Congratulations!

_____

receives this award for

_____

Signed _____ Date _____

© Carson-Dellosa

Congratulations!

_____

receives this award for

_____

Signed _____ Date _____

© Carson-Dellosa

Way to Go!

_____

has completed

_____

Signed _____ Date _____

© Carson-Dellosa

Star Student!!

 _____

receives this award for

_____

Signed _____ Date _____

© Carson-Dellosa

Congratulations

_____

receives this award for

_____

Signed _____ Date _____

© Carson-Dellosa

Congratulations!

_____

receives this award for

_____

Signed _____ Date _____

© Carson-Dellosa

Star Student!

receives this award for _____

Signed _____ Date _____

© Carson-Dellosa

able	basket	angry	backyard
above	ahead	apart	bare
add	also	asleep	before
afraid	always	awake	below

beside	between	brave	breeze
build	cap	cattle	center
certain	chase	clever	climb
collect	cover	cross	different

difficult	empty	extra	follow
dine	enter	fact	frighten
dry	except	few	garage
early	exchange	final	garbage

golden	grandpa	half	homework
hope	hospital	hum	idea
invite	job	join	lady
leap	library	loose	market

meet	message	minute	neck
neighbor	nod	ocean	office
often	once	own	pair
paw	peek	perfect	piece

practice	return	scold	trap
probably	robber	sentence	twig
prove	root	sneaker	win
quilt	rush	terrible	world